The CIVIL WAR HISTORY Series

NEW HAMPSHIRE IN THE CIVIL WAR

THE **CIVIL WAR HISTORY** SERIES

NEW HAMPSHIRE IN THE CIVIL WAR

BRUCE D. HEALD, PH.D.

ARCADIA

Published by Arcadia Publishing,
an imprint of Tempus Publishing, Inc.
2A Cumberland Street
Charleston, SC 29401

Printed in Great Britain.

Library of Congress Catalog Card Number: 2001091100

For all general information contact Arcadia Publishing at:
Telephone 843-853-2070
Fax 843-853-0044
E-Mail sales@arcadiapublishing.com

For customer service and orders:
Toll-Free 1-888-313-2665

Visit us on the internet at http://www.arcadiapublishing.com

*To all New Hampshire veterans
who proudly served our nation in uniform*

CONTENTS

ACKNOWLEDGMENTS

I would like to thank the following individuals, companies, and historical societies that have made this history and material available for publication: Ashland Historical Society, Mr. and Mrs. Robert Bennett, the Florida State Archives, Stephen T. Foster, Douglas P. Knight, Beth Lavertur, Kenneth Leidner, the National Archives, New Hampshire Historical Society, New Hampshire Veterans Association, David Ruell, Sanbornton Historical Society, David Smolen, U.S. Army Military History Institute, and Rudy VanVeghten.

BIBLIOGRAPHY

The American Soldiers and Sailors in War (A Pictorial History); Edward J. Stanley, Publisher, 1898.
Battles and Leaders of the Civil War (Grant-Lee Edition), Vols. I–VI; the Century Company, New York, 1888.
Civil War in America, by John S.C. Abbott; Gurdon Bills, Springfield, Mass., 1866.
Filling the Void, by Rudy VanVeghten; the Meredith Press, Meredith, N.H., 1989.
Gettysburg, by Herbert L. Grimm and Paul L. Roy; Time News Publishing Company, Gettysburg, Pa., 1927.
Granite Monthly Publications; Concord, N.H.
Great Battles of the Civil War; Time Inc., 1961.
Harpers Pictorial:The Civil War; Harpers Brothers, New York, 1866.
The History of the Civil War in the United States, by Samuel M. Schmucker, LL.D., and L.P. Brockett, Ph.D.; Jones Brothers & Company, Chicago/St. Louis, 1865.
New Hampshire: A History, by Hobart Pillsbury; the Lewis Historical Publishing Company, New York, 1927.
New Hampshire Heritage, 1861–65; NA_Heritage@hotmail.com.
Queen of Republic, by Henry D. Northrop; the New England Education Society, Boston, 1900.
Soldiers, Sailors, Slaves, and Ships (Civil War Photography of Henry P. Moore), by W. Jeffrey Bolster and Hilary Anderson; the New Hampshire Historical Society, Concord, N.H., 1999.

INTRODUCTION

Before the start of the Civil War, fiery rhetoric abounded as to whether new territories entering the United States would be free or slave states. Debates surrounding the economic right or moral wrong of this issue as well as states' rights to secede raised the animosity between the Northern and Southern states to a fevered pitch.

In April 1861, Southerners made a decisive move as they fired on Fort Sumter, South Carolina. Enraged Northerners saw this attack as a treasonous act against the United States and a violation of the Constitution; thus, thousands of Northern volunteers, including those in New Hampshire, rushed to join the Union army.

Even as abolitionists such as William Lloyd Garrison and Frederick Douglass instilled Northerners with a compelling and moral conscience regarding the plight of slaves, Pres. Abraham Lincoln would not wage war on slavery. Still, for some, the abolition of slavery became an issue, a battle cry. "Although the war has not been waged against slavery," Secretary of State William H. Seward noted in the spring of 1862, "the army acts . . . as an emancipating crusade[r]."

Having charged the nation "to defend and maintain the supremacy of the Constitution and to preserve the Union," Lincoln felt that if the country were to break apart, the great experiment in self-government established by the founding fathers would have failed. Taking Lincoln's plea to heart, honorable and patriotic Northerners willingly left loved ones to fight for their country.

In a letter to his wife, one soldier wrote: "I have no misgivings about, or lack of confidence in the cause in which I am engaged. . . . I know how strongly American Civilization now leans on the triumph of the Government, and how great a debt we owe to those who went before us through the blood and sufferings of the Revolution. And I am willing—perfectly willing—to lay down all my joys in this life, to help maintain this Government, and to pay that debt."

The Civil War began deep in the domestic condition of our people. The family and home lay at the bottom of the contention which, beginning as far back as the adoption of the Constitution, broke into the actual violence in 1861. The domestic life of the original 13 colonies had been diverse in the last degree. Politically, the colonists had agreed on one premise, namely, that they would separate themselves from the mother country and become a nation of free men. This agreement was political and civil in character, not domestic or national. In the course of time, most of these domestic varieties were absorbed into two main types: one, the free, robust, restless, Northern family; the other, the concentrated, well-mannered, and domineering Southern family. Members of the first family rested on free labor; they all worked with their hands. Members of the second family relied on bonded service; they were aristocrats who believed in the function of capital to own labor as one of the elements of its strength and perpetuity, and in the actual and ever-present condition of slavery.

Through political cohesion and civil structure, the discordant domestic life was at length brought into a union. However, there was no assimilation and, in the course of time, conflict broke out and history decided which type of domestic life should prevail in the great central belt of North America.

Lincoln framed the war as a noble crusade to save democracy and determine its future throughout the world. His lofty concept of the war did much to mobilize the Northern states, and New Hampshire joined in that crusade. Little did anyone know or comprehend what would be the magnitude of the war and its tragic effect it would have upon the American people. Four long and bloody years followed those first shots fired on Fort Sumter.

New Hampshire men joined the ranks of the Northern states fighting to defend and preserve the Union. In 1862, Col. Edward E. Cross, 5th New Hampshire Volunteer Regiment, heroically announced at Antietam: "The enemy are in front and the Potomac River is in the rear. We must conquor this day, or we are disgraced and ruined. I expect each one will do his duty like a soldier and a brave man. Let no man leave the ranks on any pretense. If I fall leave me until the battle is won. Stand firm and fire low. Shoulder arms! Forward march!" Cross was killed in battle at Gettysburg, 1863.

In the course of those four years, New Hampshire sent 31,650 enlisted men and 836 officers into battle. Of these troops, 1,803 enlisted men and 131 officers were killed or wounded.

These chapters contain memories of New Hampshire's involvement in the Civil War, images and accounts of the battle experiences and at camp living. They are presented as a tribute to each soldier and sailor who served during this period of rebellion.

—Bruce D. Heald, Ph.D.

One

A CALL TO ARMS
THE NORTHERN CAUSE

PRELUDE. The Southern states were determined not to submit to the rule of Abraham Lincoln as president of the United States. Soon after Lincoln was elected in the fall of 1860, they took measures to form a separate government. The Northern states were loyal to Lincoln, and no state was more ably represented in Washington when Lincoln arrived to take the oath of office than was New Hampshire. John P. Hale, the foremost abolitionist in the country, and Daniel Clark of Manchester, the first Republican senator ever elected from that city, represented the state in the U.S. Senate. Gilman Marston of Exeter and Thomas N. Edwards of Keene, two of the foremost lawyers in the state, were already serving in Congress and were reelected the following year.

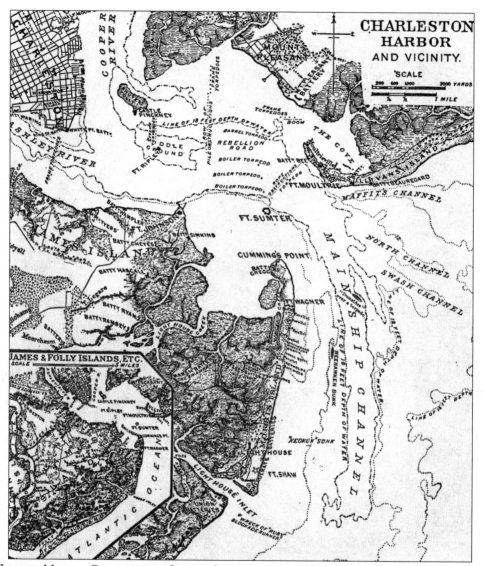

HARBOR MAP OF CHARLESTON, SOUTH CAROLINA, AND VICINITY. Located near the center of the harbor is Fort Sumter, the site of the first hostile demonstration against the national government. Initially, the steamer *Star of the West* was fired upon; it had arrived at the fort with provisions to supply Major Anderson, who was stationed there. Next came the bombardment of Fort Sumter, which resulted in its capitulation to the Southern forces on April 13, 1861.

There were four batteries on Sullivan's Island between Beauregard and Fort Marshall, which was located at the eastern end of the island. They were Batteries Bee, Marion, Moultrie, and Rutledge, close to Fort Moultrie, on the east. Seccessionville, near the center of James Island, appears on the map of James and Folly Islands. After Cumming's Point was evacuated by the Confederates, Battery Gregg was named Putnam for New Hampshire's Col. Haldimand S. Putnam, and a work east of Battery Gregg, facing the main channel, was named Battery Chatfield, after Col. John L. Chatfield; both colonels lost their lives in the assault on Battery Wagner.

THE INTERIOR OF FORT SUMTER AFTER THE BOMBARDMENT, 1861. Shown here are the gate, the gorge wall, and one of the eight-inch columbiads set as mortars, bearing on Morris Island. The bombardment of Fort Sumter created great indignation throughout the Northern states and, on April 15, 1861, Pres. Abraham Lincoln called for 75,000 troops, to serve for three months. Thus commenced one of the greatest rebellions that ever occurred in any civilized nation, a war that continued for four years and cost the lives of more than 500,000 men.

MAJOR ANDERSON AND HIS OFFICERS AT FORT SUMTER. Officers at Fort Sumter at the time of the bombardment were, from left to right, as follows: (front row) Capt. Abner Doubleday, Maj. Robert Anderson, S.W. Crawford (surgeon), and Capt. John G. Foster of New Hampshire; (back row) Brev. Capt. Truman Seymour, Lt. G.W. Snyder, Lt. Jeff C. Davis, 2d Lt. R.K. Meade Jr., and Lt. Theodore Talbot.

MAJ. GEN. JOHN G. FOSTER (1823–1874). New Hampshire native John G. Foster witnessed the very beginning of the Civil War, at Fort Sumter with Major Anderson. The young man from Whitefield had earned two brevets in the Mexican War. A West Pointer (1846) and a career engineer, he was in charge of the engineering operations in Charleston Harbor. For his action on the night of December 26, 1860, when he helped to move the garrison of Fort Moultrie into unfinished Fort Sumter, Foster was brevetted major. During the siege of the fort, he refused to allow his engineering officers to double as line officers to aid Anderson's overworked artillery officers. Following the capitulation and brief service in Washington and Maryland, Foster was named brigadier general, U.S. Volunteers, on October 23, 1861. His commands included 1st Brigade, Burnside's North Carolina Expedition (1861–1862) and 1st Division, Department of North Carolina (1862). Foster participated in the victories at Roanoke Island, New Bern, and Fort Macon. Injured in the fall of his horse, he was out of action for several months but was given charge of operations against Charleston in May 1864. A major general of volunteers since July 18, 1862, Foster reverted to the rank of major of engineers after the war and remained in the regular service until his death. He received brevets in the regular army to major general.

STATE PARTICIPATION. New Hampshire promptly responded to the president's call by sending 35,000 men to the war. It is estimated that some 5,000 of them were slain in battle and another 5,000 died soon afterward from wounds received and diseases incurred.

New Hampshire sent 18 regiments of infantry, a regiment of cavalry, a regiment of heavy artillery, 3 companies of sharpshooters, and a squadron of New England cavalry, Dartmouth cavalry, and the New Hampshire Light Battery to the Civil War. Included in the 35,000 were more than 3,000 in the navy.

LT. COL. GILMAN E. SLEEPER, 1ST NEW HAMPSHIRE VOLUNTEER REGIMENT. Lt. Col. Gilman E. Sleeper, a native of East Kingston and a resident of Salem, was in charge of Company K field and staff, and later was an officer of the 4th New Hampshire Volunteer Regiment, Company K. He enlisted at the age of 30 on April 27, 1861, as a private. He was appointed captain on April 30, 1861, mustered in on May 7, 1861, and mustered out on August 9, 1861. He mustered in the 4th Regiment on September 18, 1861, as captain. He was appointed lieutenant colonel on May 16, 1862, and was discharged on November 27, 1863.

On May 1, 1861, the 1st New Hampshire Regiment of U.S. Volunteers was organized and mustered in at Concord for three months' service and, by May 25, 1861, was armed and equipped for the field. Additional officers of the regiment included Col. Mason W. Tappen of Bradford, Lt. Col. Thomas J. Whipple of Laconia, Maj. Aaron F. Stevens of Nashua, and Adj. Enoch Q. Fellows of Sandwich.

CAPT. FREDERICK A. KENDALL, 1ST NEW HAMPSHIRE VOLUNTEER REGIMENT. Capt. Frederick A. Kendall, a native of Concord, enlisted on August 20, 1861, as private. He was appointed second lieutenant on September 20, 1861, Company I and Company B. He later became an officer in the 4th New Hampshire Volunteer Regiment, Company B, and then the 11th Indiana enviable Company L, Heavy Artillery USCT, the 25th and 40th U.S. Infantry. If, as a regiment, its history is meager, its individual members have a record. No less than 500 members reenlisted in subsequent military organizations. The 1st was represented in every regiment and every military organization of New Hampshire. Many of them sealed their loyalty and patriotism with their blood or returned disabled for life. After the regiment's tour of duty, members were mustered out at Concord on August 9, 1861; however, many of the officers and enlisted men continued their service by joining other New Hampshire regiments.

MAJ. CHARLES W. SAWYER, 1ST NEW HAMPSHIRE VOLUNTEER REGIMENT. Maj. Charles W. Sawyer was in charge of Company A, field and staff, and was an officer in the 4th New Hampshire Volunteer Regiment, Company B. He was born in Dover. At the age of 28, he was mustered in on May 2, 1861, as a first lieutenant, and was mustered out on August 9, 1861. Although the 1st New Hampshire Volunteer Regiment did not see much fighting, its duties were arduous. Members were active on picket duty on the Potomac, the larger portion of the time on the Maryland side of the river.

HARPER'S FERRY, MARYLAND HEIGHTS, FROM LOUDON HEIGHTS, VIRGINIA. The first complement to go from New Hampshire was the 1st Volunteer Regiment, whose members enlisted for three months in response to the proclamation issued on April 16, 1861, by Pres. Abraham Lincoln. Major Sturtevant, Concord's city marshall, put up a recruiting tent in back of the statehouse. More than 2,000 men responded. The first regiment was completed and the rest went into the second regiment. These men were obtained in five days; every 30 days thereafter, 1,000 men were sent until 16 regiments were raised and sent out of the state. On May 1, 1861, the troops were mustered in and, on May 25, they were sent to Washington, D.C.

In May 1861, Harper's Ferry was taken over by Confederate state forces and, on July 21, the 1st New Hampshire Volunteer Infantry was ordered to move its troops to that location. However, no action occurred and, on August 2, the troops were ordered back to New Hampshire and were mustered out on August 9, 1861. The 1st never saw any action during the unit's three-month commission.

Philosophically, Harper's Ferry may be regarded as the opening scene of the Civil War. There, a deed of lawless patriotism was enacted, the echo of which was to resound around the world.

15

COL. HENRY A.V. POST, 2ND NEW HAMPSHIRE VOLUNTEER REGIMENT. Col. Henry A.V. Post was the first commander of the 2nd New Hampshire Volunteer Regiment and a member of Berdan's U.S. Sharpshooters. The regiment had on its roll more than 3,000 names. The additional officers of this regiment were Gilman Marston of Exeter, colonel; Francis S. Fisk of Keene, lieutenant colonel; Josiah Stevens Jr. of Concord, major; Samuel G. Langley of Manchester, adjutant; John S. Goodfrey of Hampton Falls, quartermaster; and Henry E. Parker of Concord, chaplain.

A large proportion of the original members of the regiment were enlisted for three months' service under President Lincoln's first call, many of them among the earliest recruits in April 1861. However, early in May, while the regiment was still in camp at Portsmouth, orders were received from the War Department to send no more three months' troops. Most of the men thereupon enlisted for three years, this second muster by companies dating from June 1 to 8. The regiment left Portsmouth on June 20, arriving at Boston on the same day and at New York on the June 21.

THE 2ND NEW HAMPSHIRE VOLUNTEER REGIMENT. This regiment went into camp at Portsmouth and arrived on the field just in time to participate in the First Battle of Bull Run. The 2nd Regiment, being the first in the field of battle, saw more service than any other, being nearly all the time in Virginia, where more blood was spilled than in any other state in the union. The 2nd marched over 6,000 miles, participated in nearly 30 battles, and lost 1,000 men.

The roll of the 2nd Regiment, during its organization, contained more than 3,000 names. Every regiment but two from the state was supplied in part with officers from its ranks; and more than 30 regiments in the field had upon their rosters names of men who were once identified with it.

THE FIRST BATTLE OF BULL RUN CAMPAIGN, JULY 21, 1861. The first important battle of the war was fought on Sunday, July 21, 1861, near Manassas Junction, about 30 miles west-southwest of Washington, D.C. Here, a Confederate army numbering about 22,000 men and commanded by General Beauregard, held a line eight miles long between the Alexandria Railroad and the Warrenton Turnpike. The 2nd New Hampshire Regiment opened the fight at the First Bull Run. A national army (Union) of 28,000 men with 49 guns and a battalion of cavalry, commanded by Gen. Irvin McDowell, moved out from Washington to attack. Because the national capital was full of spies, the Confederate commander knew exactly what to expect. After a preliminary affair at Blackburn's Ford on July 18, the Union army crossed the stream and fell upon the left flank of the enemy with the purpose of seizing a point on the Manassas Gap Railroad to prevent the arrival of Confederate reinforcements.

The chief battleground was a wooded plateau on the banks of Bull Run and, here, the battle was conducted skillfully on both sides. Every field officer of one Alabama regiment was disabled, and the Confederate Generals Bartow and Bee were killed. As the Confederates were driven back, the Union forces, in following, became separated and, fighting in detachments, lost their advantage.

The First Battle of Bull Run, "The Rout of Union Troops," July 21, 1861. In the afternoon, 5,000 fresh troops under Gen. J.E. Johnston, arrived by rail from Shenandoah Valley. The Union flank, which had been counting on General Patterson's force to hold Johnston at Shenandoah, was thrown into a panic, disrupting Gen. Irvin McDowell's army, which streamed back to Washington in wild disorder.

The following is Stephen T. Foster's account of Gen. J.E. Johnston's arrival on the field to reinforce the Confederate line: "Around 2:00 P.M., Union commander Gen. Irving McDowell sent two batteries forward to within 300 yards of the Rebel line, where they began firing to soften it up before the Union infantry attacked. A Rebel Virginia regiment dressed in blue headed straight for the Union batteries, but the gunners thought they were Union troops and held their fire until it was too late. At a distance of 70 yards, the Rebels discharged a volley, killing and wounding many of the Union gunners. Then the Rebels charged and captured the cannon, while surviving gunners and their infantry support fled back the way they had come, demoralizing the green troops moving up to the battle. Taking advantage of the Union setback, Gen. Thomas J. Jackson ordered his Virginia brigade to charge."

The Confederate loss in this action was about 1,900; the Union loss, about 1,500 killed or wounded and 1,500 captured.

Col. Gilman Marston of Exeter was severely wounded in this battle, and the regiment's loss was reported as 7 killed, 56 wounded, and 46 missing.

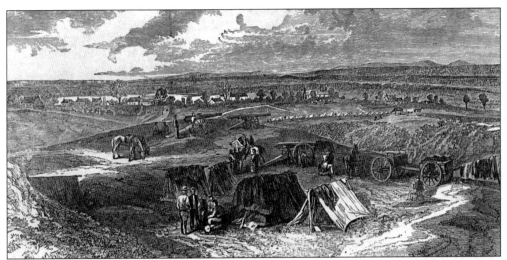

A VIEW OF THE BATTLEFIELD OF SECOND BULL RUN, AUGUST 1863. Artist Edwin Forbes provided this sketch of the battlefield. The line of the Manassas Railroad had by this time been completely occupied by the Union forces. The Army of Northern Virginia had withdrawn into the interior, and the contested ground here delineated was reoccupied, never to be lost again. Henceforth, the limits of the Confederacy contracted more and more, until, in less than two years, it was reduced to two points, at Appomattox and Raleigh. The aspect of war here shown has become almost pastoral in its simplicity and peacefulness. The great guns and caissons are the only remaining symbols of the dreadful conflict that rent the country. During this battle, the 2nd Regiment lost 36 men.

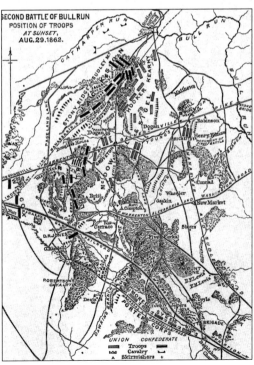

A MAP OF THE SECOND BATTLE OF BULL RUN, POSITION OF TROOPS AT SUNSET, AUGUST 29, 1862. This map illustrates the situation at the time of the greatest success on the right, when Jackson's left had been turned upon itself by Kearny's, Reno's, and Hooker's division.

On February 26, 1863, the 2nd Regiment was ordered back to Concord. The troops were assigned duty at Fort Constitution in Portsmouth until May 25. Then they were assigned to duty in Washington, D.C., where they stayed until June 11, 1863, when the regiment rejoined the Army of the Potomac and proceeded to Gettysburg, Pennsylvania.

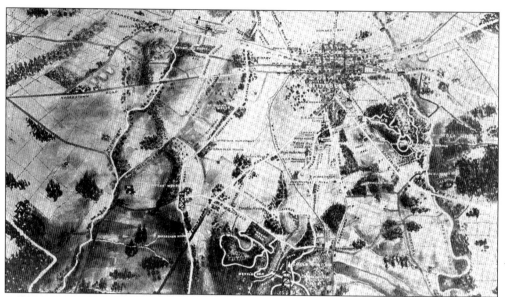

A MAP OF THE GETTYSBURG BATTLEFIELD, JULY 1863. This map shows the exact location of the most interesting places of battle from a historical viewpoint. In the lower center is Devil's Den, Round Top, and Little Round Top.

THE BATTLE OF GETTYSBURG, "LITTLE ROUND TOP AND DEVIL'S DEN." On July 2, 1863, the Confederate forces made an oblique attack on the Union position at Gettysburg. This attack brought Gen. John B. Hood's division of Gen. James Longstreet's corps into first contact with the south and east sides of the exposed position of the Union III Corps of the far left of the Union line. Gen. Evander Law's Alabama brigade moved toward the high hill known as Round Top while Gen. Jerome Robertson's brigade of Texans and Arkansans drove toward the jumble of large boulders known as Devil's Den. The area between these two positions, which became known as the "Slaughter Pen," was littered with bodies of Rebels who were felled by devastating volleys of rifles and canister before the New Hampshire Yankee pulled back to the Devil's Den.

A GETTYSBURG CAMPAIGN, "THREE DAYS OF CARNAGE." The inevitable clash between these two great American armies saw three days of horror, sacrifice, and bravery resulting in more than 50,000 casualties and the defeat of the Confederate army. Shown are the Confederate soldiers who held to the fire of the Union. The highest casualties of the 2nd Regiment came at Gettysburg, with 47 men losing their lives.

THE DEAD AT DEVIL'S DEN, GETTYSBURG. These sharpshooters lay prone beside the mossy boulders and scrub trees of the Devil's Den. They paid the ultimate price for the Union.

"DEVIL'S DEN—A NATIONAL CEMETERY IN ITSELF." This young sharpshooter was one of thousands who gave their life for a cause. In their lonely fastness, these Confederate boys sent many a swift message of death into the Union lines fighting on the nearby crest. Suddenly, a Yankee shell bursting over this young soldier wounds him in the head but is not merciful enough to kill him outright. The musket, rusted by many storms, still leans against the rock; the remains of the Rebel soldier lie undisturbed.

THE BATTLE OF COLD HARBOR, "STALEMATE," JUNE 1 TO 3, 1864. On May 27, 1864, the 2nd New Hampshire Regiment, under the command of Gen. Ulysses S. Grant, planned a massive assault on the Rebel lines at Cold Harbor. The six Union divisions struck Anderson's four divisions shortly after 5:00 p.m. on June 2 and came close to carrying the Rebel position before being beaten back with a loss of 2,200 casualties. Of these casualties, New Hampshire's 2nd had a loss of 36 men.

THE SIEGE OF PETERSBURG, VIRGINIA, JUNE 16, 1864, TO APRIL 2, 1865, A BATTLE BEYOND HUMAN ENDURANCE. The 2nd Regiment was detached from the brigade on June 9, 1864, and was assigned to duty at corps headquarters until August 13 of that year. On June 15, 1864, the troops served duty in the trenches before the assault on Petersburg. "Every step we advanced, the greatest slaughter," wrote a member of the Union army about the dawn attack on the Confederates at Petersburg on June 18, 1864. For three days, the Union troops had been banging away at the Rebel lines before Petersburg, and though they had come very close, they had never been able to break through the outnumbered Southerners' stubborn defense.

By evening, an entire Confederate corps had entered the earthworks, and Union army commander Ulysses S. Grant, realized that he had lost his chance to slip past the Rebels and capture Richmond. He had sacrificed 10,000 men in four days of attack. Now, he began a siege.

The 2nd Regiment was involved in 22 engagements. The highest casualties came at Gettysburg, 47; Second Bull Run, 36; and Williamsburg, 21 men. The totals for the 2nd Regiment were 2,555 casualties and 178 deaths. The regiment was mustered out on December 19, 1865.

VOLUNTEERS
WANTED!

E Pluribus *Unum.*

In pursuance of a Proclamation by
the President of the U.States, and by order of the Gov. of N.H. the

Third Regiment of Volunteers
within the State of New-Hampshire, will be enlisted for three years,
unless sooner discharged by proper authority, to be held in readiness for service when
ever called for.

In accordance with the above, and acting under the orders of th
Governor of this State, I have opened a

RECRUITING OFFICE
AT

UNION-HALL BUILDING, COR. MARKET & HANOVER STS.
PORTSMOUTH,

for the enlistment for three years, of able-bodied men. None will be received who ar
under the age of eighteen, or over the age of forty-five. All under 21 will be required t
bring a written consent from their Parents or Guardians.

Volunteers who shall be accepted will be uniformed, armed and equipped, whe
mustered into the service, at the expense of the State, and their pay will be the same a
that of the corresponding rank in the Army of the United States, to commence at th
date of enlistment.

GEORGE W. TOWLE, Recruiting Officer

PORTSMOUTH, N. H. July 22, 1861.

WANTED POSTER, PORTSMOUTH, JULY 22, 1861. The 3rd New Hampshire Volunteer
Infantry was organized at Concord and was mustered in on August 23, 1861, for a three-
year commission.

COL. ENOCH Q. FELLOWS, COMMANDER OF THE 3RD NEW HAMPSHIRE VOLUNTEER REGIMENT, AUGUST 1861 TO JUNE 1862. Col. Enoch Q. Fellows, a native of Sandwich, enlisted at the age of 36 as a colonel on August 10, 1861. He was mustered in on August 26, 1861, and was discharged on June 28, 1862. This regiment included the following additional officers: Lt. Col. John H. Jackson of Portsmouth, Maj. John Bedel, and surgeon A.A. Moulton.

SGT. DANIEL ELDREDGE, COMPANY K, 3RD NEW HAMPSHIRE VOLUNTEER REGIMENT. A resident of Lebanon, Sgt. Daniel Eldredge enlisted on August 2, 1861. He survived dysentery and two wounds in the foot at Fort Wagner, South Carolina, in 1863, and received a wound in the left forearm at Deep Bottom Run in 1864. During the last months of the war, he ran an induction center in New Hampshire. He was discharged on May 21, 1865, as a first lieutenant.

LINE OFFICERS, 3RD NEW HAMPSHIRE VOLUNTEER REGIMENT, HILTON HEAD, SOUTH CAROLINA, MARCH TO APRIL 1862. A group of line officers of the 3rd Regiment is shown at Hilton Head, South Carolina. On the left, sitting on the drum, is Captain Henderson. On his left sit Lieutenants Miles and Cody; Captains Donohoe, Carleton, Emmons, and Wiggins; and Chaplain Henry Hill. Bandmaster Ingalls is on the right.

HEADQUARTERS, COMPANY B, 3RD NEW HAMPSHIRE VOLUNTEER REGIMENT, HILTON HEAD, SOUTH CAROLINA, MARCH TO APRIL 1862. At headquarters are, from left to right, Captain Ayers, and Lieutenants Fogg and Jackson. This regiment performed meritorious service in South Carolina and Virginia. The troops were in many hard-fought battles and suffered heavy losses in some of them. The regiment actively served at James Island, Fort Wagner and its siege, Drury's Bluff, Half-way House, Bermuda Hundred, Deep Run, and other places. At the Battle of Fort Wagner, the regiment lost 104 men and at Deep Run, 93 men. The 3rd stood high in the service as a brave and efficient regiment and was an honor to the state of New Hampshire. The regiment was mustered out on July 20, 1865.

The 3rd was involved in 24 engagements. The highest casualties came at Drury's Bluff, 66 men, and Seccessionville, 26 men. The totals for the 3rd Regiment were 1, 769 casualties and 148 deaths.

COL. THOMAS J. WHIPPLE, 4TH NEW HAMPSHIRE VOLUNTEER REGIMENT. Col. Thomas J. Whipple was born in Wentworth and was a resident of Laconia. He enlisted at the age of 45 as colonel on August 20, 1861, mustered in on September 18, 1861, and resigned on March 18, 1962.

The 4th New Hampshire Volunteer Regiment was organized in Manchester and was mustered into service in September 1861. Other officers of the 4th included Lt. Col. Louis Bell of Farmington, Maj. Jeremiah D. Drew of Salem, Adj. Henry W. Fuller of Concord, and John L. Kelley of Manchester, quartermaster. When the regiment left New Hampshire, it went first to Washington and then proceeded to camp near Bladensburg Toll-gate.

LT. COL. LOUIS BELL, 4TH NEW HAMPSHIRE VOLUNTEER REGIMENT. Col. Louis Bell was born in Chester to one of New Hampshire's historic families and was a resident of Farmington. He enlisted at the age of 24 as a lieutenant colonel on September 3, 1861. He was mustered in on September 18, 1861, and was appointed colonel on May 16, 1862. After serving nobly for nearly four years, he was one of the brave who fell at Fort Fisher in the hour of victory. He died on January 16, 1865.

27

THE BATTLE SCENE OF PORT ROYAL, OCTOBER 1861. On November 29, 1861, the 4th New Hampshire Regiment arrived at Port Royal, South Carolina. It remained in South Carolina for approximately three months and then sailed for Fernandina, arriving there on March 5, 1862. In late October 1861, Samuel F. DuPont, flag officer, assembled a fleet of 75 warships, with 12,000 troops in transport. Their objective was Port Royal Sound, which was guarded by an earthwork on each side on the harbor entrance—Fort Beauregard at Bay Point and Fort Walker on Hilton Head Island. On April 1863, the 4th moved on siege operations against Morris Island and against Forts Wagner and Gregg. Later, on September 7, 1863, they were involved in the capture of Forts Wagner and Gregg.

THE EVACUATION OF FORT WAGNER, "SIEGE TACTICS," SEPTEMBER 7, 1863. Morris Island, in the south side of Charleston Harbor, seemed to be the key to capturing the place where the Civil War began. From the northern end of Morris Island, Gen. Quincy Gillmore reasoned, his rifled cannon could pulverize Rebel-held Fort Sumter—1,400 yards away in the middle of the harbor—and force it and Charleston, the city it protected, to surrender. On July 10, 1863, Gillmore's 11,000-man army, supported by the guns on Union ships, landed on the southern end of Morris Island and quickly took control of three quarters of it. The northern quarter was solidly in Rebel hands and was protected by Fort Wagner, one of the most formidable forts. Fort Wagner stretched 630 feet across the island with the ocean on the east, an impenetrable marsh on the west, sand walls 30 feet high, and a moat that was 50 feet wide and 5 feet deep. The only approach to the fort was across a long, narrow stretch of open beach that could be thoroughly swept by the fire of the fort's cannon. Gillmore sent three regiments racing toward the fort at dawn on July 11, 1863. Giving up on direct assaults, the Union force began siege tactics to force the surrender of Fort Wagner. The next morning the Union army walked unopposed into the fort that had held it at bay for 58 days. The situation in Charleston Harbor was unchanged by Union control of Morris Island. Fort Sumter defiantly remained in Rebel control.

MORNING DETAIL, THE 4TH NEW HAMPSHIRE VOLUNTEERS GOING TO THEIR WORK ON THE FORTIFICATIONS AT HILTON HEAD. The 4th New Hampshire belonged to Gen. Horatio G. Wright's brigade, T.W. Sherman's division, the land force that cooperated with DuPont's fleet in the reduction of Hilton Head. After its capture, Hilton Head was strongly fortified and was held by the Union authorities throughout the war.

The 4th performed valuable service in the South and was considered one of New Hampshire's best regiments. The regiment mustered out on August 23, 1865. The 4th was involved in 16 engagements. The highest casualties came at Mine Explosions, Petersburg—13 men. The totals for the 4th Regiment were 1,759 casualties and 185 deaths.

A RECRUITING POSTER OF THE 5TH NEW HAMPSHIRE VOLUNTEER INFANTRY.
"Avoid the draft! Secure a small Fortune by enlisting! All recruits to this regiment, on signing the Muster-Roll, will go at once into comfortable quarters, and receive full rations of the best the market affords, as well as a fine UNIFORM, PAY AND RATIONS commence IMMEDIATELY upon enlistment. Apply immediately to RECRUITING DEPOT."

RECRUITS WANTED!

THE UNION FOREVER!!

BOUNTY! BOUNTY!

JOIN THE

FIFTH REGIMENT, NEW-HAMPSHIRE VOLUNTEERS.

This Regiment, one of the finest in the Field from this State has won a glorious name in the Army of the Potomac on many Battle-Fields of the War, and has places for just a few good men who wish to serve their Country in her hour of need. Rally, Freemen of New-Hampshire, Rally Once Again! The Regiment is well officered, equipped, and armed with the latest model United States musket.

THE USUAL FEDERAL, STATE, AND CITY BOUNTIES!
Come on Brave Boys! Now is the time to

AVOID THE DRAFT!

Secure a small Fortune by enlisting! All recruits to this Regiment, on signing the Muster-Roll, will go at once into comfortable quarters, and receive full rations of the best the market affords, as well as a fine UNIFORM, PAY AND RATIONS commence IMMEDIATELY upon enlistment. Apply immediately to

RECRUITING DEPOT.

29

COL. EDWARD E. CROSS, LANCASTER, 5TH NEW HAMPSHIRE VOLUNTEER REGIMENT. Col. Edward E. Cross was born in Lancaster. He enlisted at the age of 31 and was appointed colonel on August 27, 1861. He organized the 5th New Hampshire Volunteer Regiment at Concord and mustered into service on October 26, 1861. He was commander of the 1st Brigade, 1st Division, 2nd Corps, Army of the Potomac (May 22–July 2, 1863). He led his regiment to the Peninsula and saw action at the Siege of Yorktown and Seven Pines. Wounded at the latter, he missed the battle of the Seven Days but returned in time to be wounded again at Antietam. Recovering, he was wounded a third time at Fredericksburg. He came through the fight at Chancellorsville without a scratch, having commanded a demi-brigade during much of the action. Two weeks later, he succeeded to command of the brigade and led it in the fighting on the second day at Gettysburg. In the fighting in the woods near Devil's Den on the Union left, he was again severely wounded. This time the wound proved to be fatal, and he died late that night, July 3, 1863.

CAPT. JAMES B. PERRY, 5TH NEW HAMPSHIRE VOLUNTEER REGIMENT, COMPANY C. Capt. James Perry of Lebanon enlisted at the age of 27 and was appointed captain on October 12, 1861. He was killed in service at Fredericksburg on December 13, 1862. Other officers in the 5th were Lt. Samuel G. Langley of Manchester; Adj. Charles Dodd of Boston; Edmund M. Webber of Somersworth, quartermaster; Luther M. Knight of Franklin, surgeon; and Elijah R. Wilkins, chaplain.

Through the winter of 1861–1862, the 5th was in the vicinity of Washington, D.C., on the Virginia side of the Potomac, doing picket and drill duty, as well as preparing for the coming spring campaign. On April 4, the regiment embarked at Alexandria for the Peninsula, landed near Ship Point, Virginia, and went through that campaign under Gen. George B. McClellan before Richmond in the summer of 1862.

OPENING OF THE BATTLE OF ANTIETAM, 1862. On September 16 and 17, 1862, the 5th Regiment served at Antietam—a very bloody two-day battle. In a report of the gallant exploit, General Sturgis said: "They rushed at a double-quick over the slope to the bridge, and over the bridge itself, with an impetuosity which the enemy could not resist, and the Stars and Stripes were planted on the opposite bank amid the most enthusiastic cheering from every part of the field."

THE MOVE TOWARD RICHMOND, VIRGINIA, APRIL 6, 1862. In April 1862, the Grand Army of the Republic, under Gen. George B. McClellen's command, began moving toward Richmond, up the Peninsula of Virginia. This army was a "flower" of the Northern States. It consisted of more than 150,000 men, exclusive of the garrisons around Washington; all were volunteers from New England and the Middle Atlantic States. They were men, said one who knew them well, who understood and appreciated the merits and values of the questions that the war was meant to answer, who believed that they were right, and who were ready to support their convictions and defend the government with their lives. The army's organization and discipline were complete, and the campaign that followed turned it into a corps of veteran soldiers equal to any in the world.

THE BATTLE OF FREDERICKSBURG, "AT THE STONE WALL," DECEMBER 13, 1862. The Battle of Fredericksburg witnessed the highest casualties of the 5th: 57 men. Around noon, a brigade of Yankees filed out of Fredericksburg, formed their battle lines, and charged toward the stone wall. They were cut to pieces by Confederate artillery and fell back before the Georgians behind the wall fired a single volley. Throughout the afternoon, Union Gen. Ambrose Burnside sent wave after wave of his infantry to the slaughter, but not before seven Union divisions had stormed the wall 14 times. The Union soldiers never penetrated the wall, but a few came as close as 50 yards.

THE BATTLE OF SEVEN PINES, OR FAIR OAKS, THE 5TH NEW HAMPSHIRE VOLUNTEER REGIMENT, MAY 31 TO JUNE 1, 1862. The 5th Regiment built a grapevine bridge across the Chickahominy River in May 1862. The bridge later saved the Union army at Fair Oaks, where the 5th first saw battle. Within four months the regiment was famous throughout the army as the "Fighting Fifth" and, in little over a year, its name became immortal in a wheatfield at Gettysburg.

THE SIEGE OF PETERSBURG, "CROSSING THE JAMES RIVER." During the early hours of July 13, 1864, the Confederates manning the trenches at Cold Harbor awoke to find the Yankee lines opposite them deserted. The enemy had simply disappeared. Grant's army was moving 12 miles south to the James River and then still farther south to Petersburg. On June 15, 1864, Grant ordered his two corps to attack the Confederate lines at Petersburg, which were held by 2,500 men. The battle was badly bungled by Grant's generals, and the Union army suffered heavy losses. This regiment sustained the greatest loss in battle of any infantry or cavalry regiment in the Union army; the total number killed or wounded was 1,051. The 5th was involved in 23 engagements, including the Siege of Petersburg. Through all the subsequent years of the war, the 5th took the front rank. The regiment was mustered out on June 28, 1865.

BRIG. GEN. SIMON G. GRIFFIN, 6TH NEW HAMPSHIRE VOLUNTEER REGIMENT. Gen. Simon G. Griffin was born in Nelson and was a resident of Concord. Enlisting at the age of 37, he was appointed lieutenant colonel on October 26, 1861, and was discharged on May 11, 1864. The 6th New Hampshire Volunteer Infantry was organized at Keene and was mustered in on November 27, 1861. Other officers listed were Col. Nelson Converse of Marlborough; Maj. Charles Scott of Peterborough; Adj. Phin P. Bixby of Concord; Alonzo Nute of Farmington, quartermaster; William A. Tracy of Nashua, surgeon; and Robert Stinson of Croydon, chaplain.

CAPT. MATTHEW N. GREENLEAF, 6TH NEW HAMPSHIRE VOLUNTEER REGIMENT, COMPANY C. Matthew N. Greenleaf, an Exeter resident, enlisted on October 10, 1861. He was mustered in on November 27, 1861, as a first sergeant and was appointed second lieutenant on April 29, 1862. Eventually, he was appointed captain of Company H, on July 1, 1863. He was wounded in service at the mine explosion in Petersburg, Virginia, and was mustered out on July 17, 1865. He later became a member of Company D, 5th Massachusetts Volunteer Militia.

THE HARD-FIGHTING 6TH NEW HAMPSHIRE, NOVEMBER 1861 TO JULY 17, 1865. Soon after the arrival of the 6th Regiment in Washington, D.C., the troops were assigned to Gen. Ambrose Burnside's division and were sent to Hatteras Inlet, North Carolina. Unaccustomed to army camp and the southern climate, the regiment was devastated by disease and numbered only 600 men when it went into its first battle at Camden, North Carolina, on April 19, 1862. Gen. Jesse Reno wrote the following of the 6th in his report: "The 6th New Hampshire had steadily advanced in line on the left of the road and when within about 200 yards, poured in a most deadly volley, which completely demoralized the enemy and finished the battle."

THE SECOND BATTLE OF BULL RUN, 1862. On August 29, 1862, the 6th Regiment was transferred to Virginia in time to participate in the Second Battle of Bull Run. On the first day of battle, the regiment attacked the Confederate line but was repulsed, losing 233 men.

THE BATTLE OF FREDERICKSBURG, DECEMBER 13, 1862. Months later, the 6th Regiment made a futile assault on the Confederate position at the base of Marye's Heights; the regiment was left with only 190 men. The charge of the Union troops upon the Confederate fortifications, exposed the men to the fire of artillery on the Heights. But shot and shell, though raking their ranks, did not stop them. On they went to a slight rise, 150 yards to the front, where they reformed, and then charged. The assault was futile, as the enemy was waiting and ready. Later, the 6th was transferred west to fight in the Vicksburg campaign.

THE BATTLE OF THE WILDERNESS, "A CRUSHING ATTACK BY LEE'S CONFEDERATES," MAY 5 TO 7, 1864. In January 1864, the unit of 288 men reenlisted for the war and received a 30-day furlough. They were back on the firing line in time for the Battle of the Wilderness and Spotsylvania. After the success of the Union assault at Orange Plank Road at dawn on May 6, 1864, the second day of battle quickly changed for the Union soldiers. While the battle raged on, Gen. Ulysses S. Grant sat calmly on a stump in the rear of the Northern lines, smoking cigars and whittling.

THE BATTLE OF SPOTTSYLVANIA, MAY 11, 1864. Throughout the cold and damp day, Grant moved his No. II Corps to a concealed position from which it could attack the apex of Mule Shoe. Over the sound of the rain, the Confederates, in the muddy Mule Shoe trenches, heard a rumble coming from the Union lines in front of them. It was the sound of 15,000 Union troops gathering in the darkness to form a massive formation 50 ranks deep.

The Union soldiers moved forward through the rain and fog and overpowered the surprised Rebel pickets. Meeting little resistance, the Union troops broke into a run and stormed over the Rebel line.

THE SIEGE OF PETERSBURG, APRIL 2, 1862. Shown is the 6th Regiment when it stormed and captured the Rebel position at Fort Damnation on the Petersburg line. The 6th was involved in 21 engagements. The highest casualties came at Second Bull Run, 66 men; Spottsylvania, 14 men; Fredericksburg, 13 men. When the regiment ended its service on July 17, 1865, only 189 men out of the original 1,000 were left to be mustered out.

Colonel H. S. Putnam 7ᵗʰ N. H. Reg.ᵗ

COL. HALDERMAN S. PUTNAM, 7TH NEW HAMPSHIRE VOLUNTEER REGIMENT. Col. Halderman S. Putnam, a native of Cornish, enlisted at the age of 25. He was appointed colonel on October 15, 1861, and was mustered in on December 15, 1861. He died in action on July 18, 1863, at Fort Wagner, South Carolina.

The 7th Regiment was organized at Manchester and was mustered in on December 15, 1861, under the supervision of Gen. Joseph C. Abbott of Manchester. Other officers of the 7th Regiment were Maj. Daniel Smith of Dover; Adj. Thomas A. Henderson of Dover; Andres H. Young of Dover, quartermaster; William W. Brown of Manchester, surgeon; and James C. Emerson of Fisherville, chaplain.

COL. J.C. ABBOTT, 7TH NEW HAMPSHIRE VOLUNTEER REGIMENT. Col. J.C. Abbott was born in Concord and was a resident of Manchester. He enlisted on October 2, 1861, as a lieutenant colonel. On July 22, 1863, he was appointed colonel and was mustered out on July 20, 1865. He succeeded the officer in command of the 7th who later became general in the Army of the Potomac. Abbott died on October 8, 1881, in Wilmington, North Carolina.

CAPT. CHARLES A. LAWRENCE, 7TH NEW HAMPSHIRE VOLUNTEER REGIMENT, COMPANY B. Capt. Charles A. Lawrence was born in New Ipswich and was a resident of Nashua. He enlisted at the age of 33 on September 30, 1861. He was mustered in on November 1, 1861, as a sergeant, was appointed captain on November 2, 1864, and was mustered out on July 20, 1865.

The 7th Regiment moved from Manchester to New York on January 16, 1862. On February 13, 1863, they sailed for Tortugas and from there went to Beaufort and finally to St. Augustine and Fernandina, Florida.

CAPT. JAMES M. CHASE, 7TH NEW HAMPSHIRE VOLUNTEER REGIMENT, COMPANY D. Capt. James M. Chase, a native of Hopkinton, enlisted at the age of 31 on September 5, 1861, as a private. He was appointed captain on November 6, 1861, was mustered in on November 6, 1861, was wounded on February 20, 1864, in Olustee, Florida, and was discharged on December 30, 1864.

In June 1863, the 7th New Hampshire Volunteer Regiment sailed for Hilton Head, South Carolina. Up to this date, the regiment had done picket, garrison, and fatigue duty during the larger portion of the time. It had lost nearly 200 men from malaria. The first battle of any importance the regiment was engaged in was the unsuccessful assault on Fort Wagner, South Carolina. In this attack Colonel Putnam, Captain Brown, and Lieutenants Baker, Cate, Bennett, and Brown were killed, and four more officers died a few days after the battle.

On December 20, 1863, the 7th Regiment was again ordered to Florida and was placed under the command of Gen. Truman Seymour. On February 20, 1864, Seymour's troops moved toward Lake City. After a march of 14 miles, they met the enemy in force at Olustee, and a fierce battle ensued in which the Northern forces were defeated.

THE BATTLE OF OLUSTEE, "A UNION DISASTER," FEBRUARY 18, 1864. Gen. Truman Seymour was in charge of this campaign, with strict orders not to advance east but simply to consolidate the gains around Jacksonville. Even though he had served valiantly through half a dozen battles and was appointed brigadier general, he had never received much recognition for his efforts and ability.

He disregarded the order not to advance and marched east with his 5,500 men in order to secure the territory between Jacksonville and the Suwannee River for the Union. Shortly after noon on February 20, near the town of Olustee, his troops came up against 5,500 Confederate militiamen commanded by Gen. Joseph Finegan. The only Civil War battle to be fought on Florida soil began quickly and lasted a short four hours. Although Finegan and his men had almost no battle experience and Seymour had the advantage in artillery, the Rebel militia soundly defeated the Union force.

Seymour lost 6 cannons, 1,600 rifles, and 1,860 men—one third of those in his command. The Confederates lost 946, killed or wounded. As a result of this Union defeat, Seymour was relieved of his command and was transferred to Virginia, where he fought admirably on many battlefields. He remained in the Union army until 1876.

THE BERMUDA HUNDRED CAMPAIGN. On May 1, 1864, the 7th Regiment was ordered to Virginia, landing at Bermuda Hundred on May 6. On May 9, Gen. Benjamin F. Butler, who was born in New Hampshire, led 14,000 Union soldiers of the James westward out of their Bermuda Hundred entrenchments to Port Walthall Junction, Virginia, and then swept south down the railroad toward Petersburg. At Swift Creek, halfway to Petersburg, they met with opposition from the Confederates. This offensive movement quickly came to a halt, whereupon Butler decided to return to the Bermuda Hundred line and mount an even stronger offensive.

Butler arranged his troops carefully, approached Drewry's Bluff slowly, and gave the Confederate troops ample time to prepare for the fight. However, the Rebels surprised the Union force with a predawn attack through the dense fog on May 16, 1864. This Rebel attack caused Butler again to order his troops to withdraw to the Bermuda Hundred peninsula.

The following day, the Confederate soldiers arrived at the Union line and began building their own fortification parallel to that of the Union, sealing the Northern troops on the small neck of land. Gen. Ulysses S. Grant was disgusted at the outcome of the offensive. "Butler's army," Grant said, "was as completely shut off from further operations against Richmond as if it had been in a bottle strongly corked." The May 16 battle of Drewry's Bluff caused 4,160 Union casualties and 2,506 Confederate casualties.

Although the 7th was not in as many battles as some of the other New Hampshire regiments, it faced the enemy with as much courage and fought with as much determination to secure victory as any regiment in the service.

The 7th was involved in 22 engagement. The highest casualties came at Olustee, Florida, 25 men. The regiment was mustered out on July 20, 1865.

BEATING THE LONG ROLL.

THE 8TH NEW HAMPSHIRE VOLUNTEER INFANTRY. The 8th Regiment was organized at Manchester and was mustered in on December 23, 1861. The officers of this regiment were Col. Hawks Fearing Jr., of Manchester; Lt. Col. Oliver W. Lull of Milford; Maj. Morill B. Smith of Concord; Orrin M. Head of Exeter, adjutant; Charles A. Putney of Manchester, quartermaster; Samuel G. Dearborn of Milford, surgeon; and Daniel P. Cilley, chaplain. On January 24, 1862, the regiment left for Boston and then sailed for Ship Mississippi on February 15, arrived there on March 15. The 8th was then attached to Gen. Benjamin F. Butler's New Orleans Expedition until March 1862; to the 1st Brigade, Department of the Gulf, until November 1862; to an independent command, Department of the Gulf, until January 1863; and to the 2nd Brigade, 3rd Division, 19th Army Corps, Department of the Gulf, until September 1863.

UNION TROOPS ATTACK PORT HUDSON. "Port Hudson will be ours today," announced Union Gen. Nathaniel P. Banks on the morning of May 27, 1863. His 30,000 troops had completely encircled the Confederate Mississippi River fortress at Port Hudson, Louisiana, a few days earlier. Banks's plan for battle called for a massive bombardment of the fort and its 7,000 Confederate defenders.

Shown here are the Union infantrymen clambering over fallen timbers during one of their attacks on the Port Hudson defenses. Thrown back with heavy losses, they cursed the entire operation, one officer fuming that "the affair was a gigantic bushwack." In the two failed attacks, the Union troops lost 4,000, dead and wounded. By mid-June, another 7,000 men had fallen ill, many suffering from dysentery or sunstroke in the stifling heat of Port Hudson's swamps. By that time, General Gardner's garrison had been reduced to 6,000 men, since some units had been sent north to help defend Vicksburg.

On the morning of June 13, all of Banks's cannons opened fire, and for an hour one shell per second rained down on Port Hudson. Having effectively demonstrated the formidable firepower on the Rebel troops, Banks then sent Gardner, the fort's commander, a demand for the surrender of his post. Gardner replied, "My duty requires me to defend this position, and therefore I decline to surrender."

THE SIEGE OF PORT HUDSON. When the surrender finally came, the men from both sides crawled from their trenches and redoubts to shake hands. Port Hudson was especially valuable to the South because its guns blocked Northern river traffic and also guarded the nearby mouth of the Red River, an avenue for goods and supplies from the west that helped sustain the Confederacy. On January 1, 1865, 341 members of the 8th Regiment formed the Veteran Battalion 8th New Hampshire Volunteer Infantry.

In total, the 8th was involved in 21 engagements. The highest casualties came at Port Hudson, 59 men, and Labadieville, Louisiana, 16 men. The regiment was mustered out on October 28, 1865.

COL. ENOCH Q. FELLOWS, 9TH NEW HAMPSHIRE VOLUNTEER REGIMENT. Col. Enoch Q. Fellows, a native of Sandwich, enlisted at the age of 37. He was appointed colonel on July 14, 1862, was mustered in on August 23, 1862, and was discharged on November 21, 1862.

The 9th New Hampshire Volunteer Regiment was recruited at Concord and was mustered in on August 15, 1862. Additional officers of the 9th were Lt. Col. Herbert B. Titus of Chesterfield; Maj. George W. Everett of New London; Adj. George H. Chandler of Concord; Carlton B. Hutchins of Lisbon, quartermaster; William A. Webster of Manchester, surgeon; and Edward M. Gushee of Dover, chaplain.

CAPT. ANDREW J. STONE, 9TH NEW HAMPSHIRE VOLUNTEER REGIMENT. Capt. Andrew J. Stone, part of the IX Corps, was a native of Dunbarton. On August 5, 1862, at the age of 33, he was mustered in as captain. He was mortally wounded in a skirmish in Federickburg, Virginia, on May 20, 1864. His regiment lost 184 men at Spottsylvania, most of them in the fight on May 12, 1864.

THE BATTLE OF SOUTH MOUNTAIN, SEPTEMBER 1862. The 9th Regiment arrived in the vicinity of Washington about the time Gen. John Pope was falling back and Gen. Robert E. Lee was pressing on with his victorious army, toward Maryland. They joined the Union troops under Gen. George B. McClellan, primarily to stop the advancement of Lee's army.

On September 14, 1862, only three weeks after leaving New Hampshire, the 9th was engaged in the Battle of South Mountain. The Confederate army was on the west side of South Mountain, which was a 50-mile-long ridge that stretched from the Potomac River into Pennsylvania. McClellan knew that three parts of Lee's army were besieging Harpers Ferry and that the rest were at Boonsboro, at the western foot of South Mountain. However, McClellan did not know the number of troops Lee had at the time.

On Sunday morning, September 14, General Hill watched the approach of four Union corps (32 brigades in 12 divisions), saying he had never "experienced a feeling of greater loneliness. It seemed as though we were deserted by all the world and the rest of mankind." Hill, however, had the advantage: a good defensible position. Each side suffered about 1,800 casualties.

THE BATTLE OF FREDERICKSBURG, "CROSSING THE RIVER." Union artillery fired across the Rappahannock River at Confederate troops who were hiding in the building and behind the walls along the waterfront of Fredericksburg, Virginia. On December 11, 1862, the Rebel sharpshooters had stalled the Union offensive by running off the engineers who had worked through the night building pontoon bridges. Suddenly, 36 Union cannons blasted away for an hour at the Confederate lines.

Admitting that his artillery fire could accomplish little more than the destruction of the town, Union army commander Gen. Ambrose Burnside ordered three regiments to be rowed across the river in pontoon boats to clear out the snipers. During this battle, the 9th Regiment suffered heavy losses. After the Battle of Fredericksburg, it continued on to Kentucky and Tennessee and won an enviable reputation in the discharge of provost and garrison duty. From Kentucky, the 9th went down the Mississippi and landed near Vicksburg.

45

THE CHARGE OF THE SECOND DIVISION INTO THE CRATER, THE EXPLOSION OF THE MINE, PETERSBURG. In the spring of 1864, the 9th Regiment again joined the Army of the Potomac and took part in all the battles from Spottsylvania Court House through to the front of Petersburg, Virginia, and in all battles before that city, up to the celebrated mine explosion. A well-organized advance on Cemetery Hill would have been a success; however, the only result of the crater mine episode was the loss of 4,000 Union soldiers and the blowing up of a few sleeping Confederates.

THE ARMY AWAITS ORDERS TO ADVANCE AFTER THE EXPLOSION OF THE MINE, PETERSBURG, JULY 30, 1864. Here, the Union troops, including the 9th Regiment, are seen at rest while en route to Poplar Springs Church. The 9th was involved in 19 engagements. The highest casualties came at Spottsylvania, 62 men; the mine explosion at Petersburg, 23 men; and Polar Springs Church, 17 men. The total number of deaths was 243. The recruits to the 9th were transferred to the 6th Regiment on June 1, 1865. Original members of the 9th were mustered out on June 10, 1865.

COLD HARBOR, THE SCENE OF STONEWALL JACKSON'S FLANK MOVEMENT AND GRANT'S OPERATION. The 10th New Hampshire Volunteer Regiment, organized at Manchester, was mustered in on September 4, 1862. The officers were Col. Michael T. Donohoe of Manchester; Lt. Col. John Coughlin of Manchester; Maj. Jesse F. Angell of Manchester; William H. Cochran of Goffstown, adjutant; Thomas Sullivan of Nashua, quartermaster; and John Ferguson of Manchester, surgeon. The first battle of Cold Harbor was fought on June 27, 1862, when Gen. George B. McClellan was on the peninsula trying to get to Richmond. The second battle was fought on June 1, 1864, when Gen. Ulysses S. Grant's forces were moving southeast toward the James River. The significance of the name of this place has been much discussed. It is an old English term meaning a house of entertainment where travelers can be provided with shelter but not with fire. Here, we see the troops approaching the farmhouse at Cold Harbor.

THE BATTLE OF COLD HARBOR. In the 30 days since hostilities had opened in the wilderness, the Union army had suffered casualties averaging 2,000 men a day, half as many men as it had lost in the previous three years of the war and twice the Rebel losses. In the fateful June attack, the Union lost over 7,000 men, five for each Confederate put out of action. "I regret this assault more than any one I ordered," announced General Grant. However, his regrets did little to help the thousands of wounded Union soldiers lying between the lines. Those lying on the field were all Union soldiers, and for four nights and three days, they lay under the blistering southern sun without food, water, or medical aid—and they died. "Grant's slaughter pen," was the name the men called the field. When Union search parties finally went out on the morning of June 7, they found only two men left alive. The 10th Regiment was involved in 18 engagements. The highest casualty count came at Cold Harbor, 23 men. The 10th's total came to 132 deaths. Recruits to the 10th were transferred to the 2nd Regiment on June 21, 1985. Original members of the 10th were mustered out on June 21, 1865.

COL. WALTER HARRIMAN OF WARNER AND LT. COL. MOSES COLLINS OF EXETER, 11TH NEW HAMPSHIRE VOLUNTEER INFANTRY. The additional senior officers of the 11th New Hampshire Volunteer Infantry were Maj. E.W. Farr of Littleton; James F. Briggs of Hillsborough, quartermaster; Charles R. Morrison of Nashua, adjutant; Jonathan S. Ross of Somersworth, surgeon; and Frank K. Stratton of Hampton, chaplain.

CAPT. CHARLES O. BRADLEY, 11TH NEW HAMPSHIRE VOLUNTEER REGIMENT. On September 2, 1862, the 11th New Hampshire Voluntary Regiment was organized and was mustered in at Concord. Later that month, the regiment left Concord and was placed in defense around the capital in Washington, D.C. Later still, it was attached to Brigg's Brigade. The first battle of note was that of Frederickburg. In the spring of 1863, the troops were ordered to Kentucky. They remained in Kentucky until June 2, when they sailed for Vicksburg and were engaged in that siege until July 4, 1863.

In the spring of 1864, the 11th again joined the army of the Potomac in Virginia, under General Grant. The troops were engaged in all the battles in their march to Richmond.

THE BATTLE OF THE WILDERNESS, MAY 6, 1864. General Grant's idea was that the proper object of attack was not Richmond but Lee's army, and his purpose was to follow that wherever it went and attack it as often as possible—to force the fighting from the start. Losses on both sides had been very heavy and, to add to the horror, the woods were set on fire by the shooting. Literally thousands were killed and many more thousands were wounded and lost in the maze of woods. May 7, 1864, was quiet except for cavalry engagements, but on May 8, Grant moved by the flank and began aggressive movements, which brought on the battle of Spottsylvania and ultimately carried him to the threshold of the Confederate capital.

THE BATTLE OF THE WILDERNESS, "BUSHWHACKING," MAY 5 TO 7, 1864. Early in the morning, Confederate troops led by Gen. Robert E. Lee advanced from the west down two parallel roads and hit the Union in the flank as it was streaming south through the Wilderness. "Up through the trees rolled dense clouds of battle smoke, circling about the green of the pines and mingling with the white of the flowering dogwoods. Underneath men ran to and fro, firing, shouting, stabbing with bayonets, beating each other with the butts of their guns," wrote a Union captain.

CAPT. LEANDER W. COGSWELL, 11TH NEW HAMPSHIRE VOLUNTEER REGIMENT. Capt. Leander W. Cogswell, a native of Henniker, enlisted at the age of 36 on August 13, 1862. Appointed captain on September 4, 1862, he was appointed lieutenant colonel on August 20, 1864, and he was discharged on April 26, 1865, as captain.

Shortly before 2:00 p.m., eight hours late, Gen. Ambrose Burnside's IX Corps arrived to support the Union troops on the Orange Plant road. However, it was the Confederates who were doing the attacking. As the Northern Yankee approached, three Rebel brigades swung north to meet them. Cogswell described the savage encounter in his 1871 regimental history: "The 11th had the advantage of the brigade, and when the center was reached a line of battle was formed, and an advance was made until the 3rd Division was reached, the men of which were lying upon the ground, hesitating to advance. The order came for the 2nd Brigade to advance, which it did in the face of a terrible, murderous fire, the bullets raining upon the men like hailstones. Just as the order came, 'Charge!' Lt. Col. Collins was shot through the head, a bullet entering his forehead, and he fell dead. On went the brave men of the 11th with such an impetuosity that the first intrenchments were carried, and many prisoners captured. The woods were on fire, the smoke was dense, the work of no other regiment could be seen . . . and still the men, flushed with success, moved on, until ascertaining themselves to be far in advance of any other regiment, Colonel Harriman called halt. . . .

"The only wonder is that more of the men were not captured. Sgt. Edmunds of Company D, and [myself] were the last men who saw Col. Harriman before his capture. When Col. Harriman was captured . . . many bullets whizzed about his head as he was seen when the smoke lifted.

"Colonel Harriman could not help falling into the hands of the enemy—as many another one did—for at this point the rebels fairly swarmed, and had the Eleventh Regiment not commenced to fall back when it did, hardly a man could have escaped capture."

A DISTANT VIEW OF THE BATTLE OF SPOTTSYLVANIA COURT HOUSE, MAY 12, 1864. The battle of Spottsylvania immediately followed that of the Wilderness, and was a part of General Grant's policy to continue hammering at Lee's army—"fighting it out on this line." Here, more men were killed and disabled in the single 24 hours of hand-to-hand fighting than in the day's battle of the Wilderness.

THE UNION ARMY ENTERING RICHMOND, VIRGINIA, APRIL 3, 1865, AND RECEPTION OF THE TROOPS ON MAIN STREET. After Grant defeated Lee at Five Forks and ordered a general advance to secure the final fruits of victory, Lee telegraphed Confederate president Jefferson Davis that he must abandon his position or be destroyed. The evacuation of Richmond began. Here, we witness the federal troops entering the city—there was cause for welcoming them, even for the whites. For the blacks, it was indeed the day of deliverance for which they had been praying.

This regiment was considered one of the best in service. It was involved in 19 engagements. The recruits to the 11th were transferred to the 6th Regiment on June 1, 1865. Original members of the 11th were mustered out on June 4, 1865. The total number of deaths was 167. The highest casualties came at Fredericksburg, 40, and Spottsylvania.

THE FIELD AND LINE OFFICERS OF THE 12TH NEW HAMPSHIRE VOLUNTEER REGIMENT. On August 10, 1862, the governor of New Hampshire gave permission and issued recruiting papers to raise a regiment in Belknap and Carroll Counties, provided it could be done in 10 days. Within six days from the date of the recruiting papers, the adjutant general of the state was notified that 10 full companies had been raised. The 12th Regiment was mustered in on September 10, 1862. The troops encamped at Concord for drill prior to leaving for the war.

The officers of the 10th Regiment were Col. Joseph H. Potter of Concord; Lt. Col. John F. Marsh of Hudson; Maj. George D. Savage of Alton; Daniel S. Bedee of Meredith, adjutant; Isaac Winch of Meredith, quartermaster; H.B. Fowler of Bristol, surgeon; Charles W. Hunt of Laconia, assistant surgeon; and Thomas L. Ambrose of Ossipee, chaplain.

MAJ. EDWARD E. BEDEE, 12TH NEW HAMPSHIRE VOLUNTEER REGIMENT. Born in Sandwich, this Meredith resident enlisted in Company I, 12th Regiment, New Hampshire Volunteers, on August 18, 1862, at the age of 24. After training at Camp Belknap, the 12th left New Hampshire on September 26, 1862.

Maj. Edward E. Bedee and his comrades participated in many of the major battles of the rebellion, including Chancelorsville, Gettysburg, and Cold Harbor. Many of the 1,400 soldiers in the regiment were killed during the war. Bedee was twice wounded in battle but recovered and returned to the front.

THE BATTLE OF CHANCELLORSVILLE, VIRGINIA, MAY 1, 1863. For more than two years, the Confederates had held their own. The opening of the military season of 1863 found them firmly planted on the line of the Rappahannock—a mere post office in Spottsylvania County, Viginia. It was 55 miles from the Confederate capital. The Union army was superior in number (132,000 men); the Confederates numbered only 65,000. Here it was that Jackson outflanked and turned the Union right, sweeping everything before him; here it was that he fell under a mistaken volley from his own lines. The battle was a defeat for the Union. General Hooker lost more than 16,000 men, and the Confederate loss was more than 12,000. The Union army withdrew across the Rappahannock, and Lee soon began his invasion of the North. On May 3, 1863, Hooker repulsed the attack of the Confederates. The great battle of Chancellorsville was fought on the evening of May 2, 1863, but more desperately on the following day. The celebrated foot cavalry was repulsed. This scene of the battle is shown above in a sketch by Edwin Forbes.

THE BATTLE OF GETTYSBURG, THURSDAY EVENING, JULY 2, 1863, FROM ROCKY HILL. There was never a more critical sunset in America than that on July 2, 1863. On the next day, the political fate of the American republic would be put into the balance of destiny. The fighting on that day had been favorable to the Confederates. They had won nearly all along the line. The Union troops were concentrating and confirming themselves on the line of the Round Tops, Cemetery Ridge, and Culp's Hill. This sketch—drawn on the evening before the great battle, on the left of Meade's position—looks to the southwest, where the long lines of Longstreet, Hill, and Johnson were ready for the next day's contest. The 12th Regiment had seen hard fighting and did honor to themselves and the state of New Hampshire. The 12th was involved in 13 engagements. Its recruits were transferred to the 2nd Regiment on June 21, 1865. The 12th sustained 180 casualties and 146 deaths. The highest casualties came at Chancellorsville, 72 men, Cold Harbor, 63 men, and Gettysburg, 26 men.

COL. AARON STEVENS, COMMANDER, 13TH NEW HAMPSHIRE VOLUNTEER INFANTRY COMPANY C. Col. Aaron Stevens, born in Derry and a resident of Nashua, enlisted at the age of 41 on August 26, 1862. He was mustered in as colonel on September 23, 1862, and was discharged on February 4, 1865.

The 13th Regiment was organized at Concord and was mustered in on September 20, 1862. The additional officers in the 13th Regiment were Lt. Col. George Bowers of Nashua; Maj. Jacob I. Storer of Portsmouth; George H. Gillis of Nashua, adjutant; Percy C. Cheeney of Peterborough, quartermaster; George B. Twitchell of Keene, surgeon; and G.C. Jones of Nashua, chaplain.

CAPT. WILLIAM J. LADD. COMPANIES B AND K, 13TH NEW HAMPSHIRE VOLUNTEER REGIMENT. Capt. William J. Ladd, a native of Portsmouth, enlisted on September 13, 1862. He was mustered in on September 30, 1862. He left Concord with the 13th Regiment for the defenses around Washington, D.C., on October 6, 1862. The regiment remained there until December 1, whereupon they moved on to Falmouth, Virginia, opposite Fredericksburg, arriving there three days prior to the Battle of Fredericksburg. On June 21, 1865, Ladd was mustered out of active service.

THE BOMBARDMENT OF FREDERICKSBURG, VIRGINIA, BY THE ARTILLERY OF THE UNION ARMY, 1862. The 13th Regiment was in the thick of the battle and lost 41 enlisted men and officers.

THE MUD MARCH. "The auspicious moment seems to have arrived to strike a great and mortal blow to the rebellion, and to gain that decisive victory which is due to the country." So announced Gen. Ambrose Burnside to his Yankee soldiers on the morning of January 20, 1863, as he started out on another great drive to beat Gen. Robert E. Lee's Army of Northern Virginia and capture the Confederate capital of Richmond, Virginia.

Here are seen the great mule-drawn wagons, carrying the pontoons. The wagons sank to their hubs; the artillery sank until only the muzzles were out of the mud. The exhausted horses floundered, as did the men; each slippery step through the ooze sucked at their shoes and weighed them down.

"The whole country was a river of mud," wrote one Yankee soldier. "The roads were rivers of deep mire, and the heavy rain had made the ground a vast mortar bed." Whole regiments and triple teams of mules hitched to the wagons and guns failed to move them. Burnside had no choice but to abandon the movement and ordered his troops back to their camps across from Fredickburg. The 13th remained at Falmouth until February 1863, when it moved with the 9th Army Corps to Newport News, Virginia. On March 13, the regiment moved to Suffolk to defend that position.

THE SECOND BATTLE OF DREWRY'S BLUFF. On May 16, 1864, the confederates launched an attack through a thick morning fog and routed the right flank of General Butler's Union troops. The Union center soon began to give way to the relentless attacks. By 10:00 a.m., Butler began withdrawing his troops just to save his army, which was quickly withering away. However, by 4:00 p.m., the Rebel forces realized that they would not be able to destroy the Union troops and had to be content with simply sending them back to their fortified base at Bermuda Hundred. During that evening, Butler's men retreated to the safety of the Peninsula. During the battle, 4,160 Union men were killed, wounded, or captured; the Confederate losses totaled about 2,500 men. The 13th was the first Union regiment to enter Richmond during the occupation of the Southern capital. The general commanding the army ordered these battles to be placed upon the national colors of the regiment. The 13th was distinguished for its daring bravery. The total number of engagements was 18. The highest casualties came at Cold Harbor, 22 men, and Petersburg, 13 men. The recruits to the 13th were transferred to the 2nd Regiment on June 21, 1865.

THE 14TH NEW HAMPSHIRE VOLUNTEER INFANTRY. This regiment was organized at Concord late in the summer of 1862 and was mustered in on September 24. The officers were Col. Robert Wilson of Keene; Lt. Col. Tileston A. Barker of Westmoreland; Maj. Samuel A. Duncan of Plainfield; Alexander Gardiner of Claremont, adjutant; William A. Hurd of Sandwich, quartermaster; William Henry Thayer of Keene, surgeon; and Elihu T. Rowe of Plainfield, chaplain. The 14th left Concord for the nation's capital in October 1862. During the fall and winter, it performed picket duty on the Potomac. In the later part of April 1863, the regiment was ordered to Washington and remained there until February 1864, doing provost duty.

THE FIGHT AT CEDAR CREEK, VIRGINIA. During their tour of duty, members of the 14th Regiment were ordered to the battles of September 19 and 22, and that of October 19 at Cedar Creek. The engagement represented here is a skirmish between Early's rear guard and Sheridan's cavalry, which harassed the retreating Confederates before they made their stand at Winchester on their way up the Shenandoah Valley with Sheridan on their heels. Through Sheridan's command, the battle was a rousing victory for the Union. During this engagement, however, the 14th Regiment lost 150 men, and 13 of its 21 officers were killed or wounded; Colonel Gardiner was mortally wounded. The 14th Regiment was not in as many battles as some of the other regiments, but it was considered a reliable regiment that performed the duties assigned it to the satisfaction of its commanders. The 14th was involved in 10 engagements. The highest casualties came at Opequan, Virginia, 54 men, and Cedar Creek, 12 men. The number of deaths totaled 159. The 14th had an average age of 27. The oldest member was 63 and the youngest was 15. The 14th was also New Hampshire's last long-term enlistment infantry unit for volunteers. The regiment was mustered out of service on July 8, 1865.

A VIEW OF COMPANY G OF THE 15TH NEW HAMPSHIRE VOLUNTEER INFANTRY IN CONCORD, 1862. The 15th Regiment was raised under the call of the president for 300,000 men, for nine months' service and was organized at Concord in the fall of 1862. The officers were Col. John W. Kingman of Durham; Lt. Col. George W. Frost of Newmarket; Maj. Henry W. Blair of Plymouth; Edward E. Pinkham of Laconia, adjutant; Ira A. Moody of Dover, quartermaster; Jeremiah F. Hall of Wolfeborough, surgeon; and Edwin M. Wheelock of Dover, chaplain. On November 13, 1862, the 15th Regiment left Concord for New York City and from there crossed the East River and encamped on the grounds of the Union racecourse in Jamaica, Long Island. The troops remained there for about three weeks until they were ordered to New Orleans in three detachments. They remained in the vicinity of New Orleans all winter, performing picket and provost duty.

THE BATTLE AT PORT HUDSON. During their time of enlistment, the members of the 15th Regiment were ordered to Port Hudson in the early summer of 1863 and remained there through the siege in the two assaults. Pictured is the Bombardment of Port Hudson by Admiral Farragut's fleet and the one-on-one combat of Union and Confederate troops at Port Hudson, Louisiana. As their time of enlistment had nearly expired, they turned over all ordnance and camp stores on July 26, 1863, and embarked on the steamer *City of Madison* for Cairo, Illinois, and thence to Chicago by rail. They arrived in Concord on August 8, 1863. All casualties occurred at the Siege of Port Hudson, 30 men. The 15th never received recruits to replenish the unit's strength. The regiment suffered a great deal from sickness. From July 31 to August 13, 16 men died; of the 741 men and officers on the roll, only 480 were fit for duty. After leaving Port Hudson for New Hampshire, 50 men were left on the way on account of sickness, many of whom died. The total death count was 115 men. A good regiment, it faithfully performed all duties assigned to it.

THE SIEGE AT PORT HUDSON, "THE CONFEDERATES HOLD ON." On December 2, 1862, the 16th New Hampshire Volunteer Regiment was organized and mustered in for nine months. Officers of the 16th were Col. James Pike of Sanbornton; Lt. Col. Henry W. Fuller of Concord; Maj. Samuel Davis Jr. of Warner; Luther T. Townsand of Salem, adjutant; Albert H. Drown of Fisherville, quartermaster; Thomas Sanborn of Newport, surgeon; and R.M. Manley of Northfield, chaplain. In November, the regiment moved to New York, joined Banks' Expeditionary Corps, and sailed for New Orleans, arriving on December 20, 1862. The unit was attached to Sherman's division, Department of the Gulf, until January 1863. Then, it was attached to the 1st Brigade, 3rd Division, 19th Army Corps, Army of the Gulf, until May 1863.

Here, at the Siege of Port Hudson, Gen. Franklin Gardner's 7,000 Confederate troops were encircled by Union Gen. Nathaniel P. Banks's 30,000-man force. The Rebels had been under siege (cut off from all supplies and reinforcements) for three weeks when, on June 13, Gardner refused Banks's demand for surrender. Banks then ordered a massive artillery bombardment of Port Hudson and resumption of the assault on the fortress early the next day. At 4:00 a.m. on June 14, wave after wave of Union troops crashed against the Confederate hold. However, the determined Rebels stood bravely at their posts and littered the ground before the fort with hundreds of dead and wounded Yankee men.

THE SIEGE AT PORT HUDSON "DISEASE & MISERY," MARCH 14 TO JULY 8, 1863. By noon the Union army had given up the contest. Of the 6,000 Union soldiers, 203 were killed, 1,401 were wounded, and 188 were missing. Of the 3,750 Confederate soldiers, 22 were killed and 25 were wounded. "One more advance," announced Banks, "and they are ours." But his men had had enough of his tactics and even threatened mutiny. There would not be "one more advance."

The 16th Regiment was involved in three engagements and sustained no casualties. The unit never received recruits to replenish its strength. Even though the regiment never lost a man in combat, disease took the lives of 213 men. The regiment was mustered out on August 20, 1863.

THE BATTLE OF GETTYSBURG, PENNSYLVANIA, JULY 1 TO 3, 1863, THE 17TH NEW HAMPSHIRE VOLUNTEER INFANTRY. The organization of the 17th Regiment commenced on November 19, 1862. It was not completed, and the two companies formed were transferred to the 2nd New Hampshire Infantry on April 16, 1863. The officers were Col. Henry O. Kent of Lancaster; Lt. Col. Charles H. Long of Claremont; Maj. George H. Bellows; George A. Wainwright of Hanover, adjutant; Edward H. Cumming, quartermaster; James D. Folsom, surgeon; and George S. Barnes, chaplain. Although the unit never faced combat, disease took the lives of four men.

After the 17th was transferred to the 2nd Regiment, one of the major battles was that in Gettysburg, Pennsylvania, from July 1 through 3, 1863. Of the 82,000 Union soldiers engaged in this battle, 3,155 were killed, 14,529 were wounded, and 5,365 were missing. The Confederate totals were 3,903 killed, 18,735 wounded, and 5,425 missing.

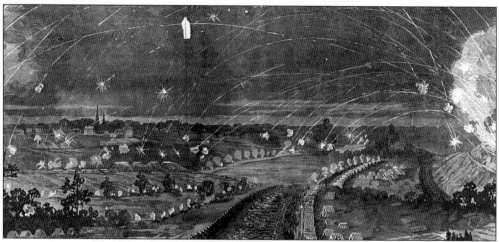

The Last Night Bombardment of Petersburg, Virginia, April 1, 1865, Preparatory for a General Assault. In 1864, the 18th New Hampshire Volunteer Regiment was organized at Concord. The commanding officers of the regiment were Col. Thomas L. Livermore of Milford; Lt. Col. J.M. Clough of New London; Maj. William I. Brown of Fisherville; George F. Hobbs of Wakefield, adjutant; Moses T. Cate of Wolfeborough, quartermaster; Samuel G. Dearborn, surgeon; and Anthony C. Hardy, chaplain.

As the war was almost over, the 18th Regiment saw relatively little. Some companies, however, fought hard before Petersburg, as illustrated in the last night bombardment of the city in the spring of 1865. The effect of the bombardment upon the city was less serious than might have been expected. Upon entering the city the next day, troops found only some of the more elevated buildings destroyed.

The 18th Regiment was involved in two engagements. The highest casualties came at Petersburg, 2, and Fort Stedman, 1. The total number of deaths was 37. After their tour of duty, six original companies were mustered out on June 10, 1865. The balance of the regiment was mustered out on July 29, 1865.

Gen. Joseph N. Clough, 18th New Hampshire Volunteer Regiment. Gen. Joseph N. Clough, a native of New London, enlisted as a lieutenant colonel on October 13, 1864. He was mustered in on October 18, 1864, for one year. Clough, originally of the 4th and later of the 18th, was considered one of the bravest men whom the state sent forth. He was mustered out on July 29, 1865.

THE NEW HAMPSHIRE BATTALION, FIRST REGIMENT NEW ENGLAND VOLUNTEER CAVALRY (1ST RHODE ISLAND VOLUNTEER CAVALRY). The officers of this battalion were Maj. David B. Nelson of Manchester and George T. Crane, adjutant. The battalion was organized in the fall of 1861 and performed fine service in the Battles of Front Royal and Gettysburg and in skirmishes in their scouting expeditions.

A major battle for this regiment was at Cedar Creek, Virginia, on August 12, 1864. The engagement represented here is a skirmish between Early's rear guard and Sheridan's cavalry, which harnessed the retreating Confederates. On January 7, 1864, all four companies—I, K, L, and M—transferred to form the 1st Regiment New Hampshire Volunteer Cavalry. This regiment was involved in 16 engagements.

The 1st Regiment New Hampshire Volunteer Cavalry was organized at Concord in the winter and spring of 1864. The officers were Col. John L. Thompson of Plymouth; Lt. Col. Benjamin T. Hutchins of Concord; Maj. Aaron Wyman of Manchester; George W. Towle of Hooksett, quartermaster; and George W. Pierce of Winchester, surgeon. This regiment was comprised of 12 companies with a total roster of 1,533 men. The 1st Cavalry was involved in 27 engagements; the highest casualties came at White Oak Swamp, 8 men.

A BATTLE SCENE AT WHITE OAKS SWAMP. The rear guard at White Oak Swamp on June 13, 1864, was Gen. W.F. Smith's division.

THE 1ST NEW HAMPSHIRE VOLUNTEER LIGHT BATTERY. This battery was organized at Manchester in August 1861. The officers were Capt. George A. Gerrish, 1st Lt. Edward H. Hobbs, and 2nd Lt. John Wadleigh. The battery left Manchester for Washington on October 31, 1861. It went into a camp of instruction for one week and immediately thereafter was assigned to the Army of the Potomac. A major battle for this battery was set at Gettysburg in July 1863.

Assigned to the 1st New Hampshire Battery were 258 men. This battery was involved in 28 engagements, including the Siege of Petersburgh, Antietam, Fredericksburg, Gettysburg, and the Wilderness. The total number of deaths was six.

ROSTER, 1ST NEW HAMPSHIRE VOLUNTEER LIGHT BATTERY, JULY 23, 1863. The 1st Company New Hampshire Volunteer Heavy Battery was organized and mustered in July 22, 1863. First stationed at Fort Constitution until May 6, 1864, the company transferred into Company A, 1st Regiment New Hampshire Volunteer Heavy Artillery on September 15, 1864. Twelve companies comprised this regiment. The officers were Col. Charles H. Long of Claremont; Lt. Col. Ira Barton of Newport; Maj. George A. Wainwright of Hanover; Ezekiel Morrill of Concord, surgeon; and C.W. Walker of Stratford, chaplain.

THE FIELD ARTILLERY. During the Civil War, field artillery consisted of cannon, howitzers, and mortars light enough to be easily transported.

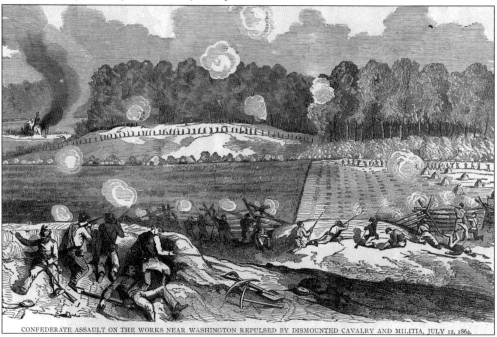

CONFEDERATE ASSAULT ON THE WORKS NEAR WASHINGTON REPULSED BY DISMOUNTED CAVALRY AND MILITIA, JULY 12, 1864.

THE CONFEDERATE ASSAULT ON THE WORKS NEAR WASHINGTON, REPULSED BY DISMOUNTED CAVALRY AND MILITIA, JULY 12, 1864. The regiment performed guard and garrison duty at the forts in Portsmouth Harbor and around the defenses at Washington. The regiment was mustered out on June 15, 1865. Recruits consolidated to two companies and were mustered out on September 11, 1865. The total enlistment of the regiment was 1,857. The number of deaths was 34.

COMPANY E, 1ST REGIMENT U.S. VOLUNTEER SHARPSHOOTERS. New Hampshire furnished three companies for this service: E, F, and G. The history of the Sharpshooters has received less than its share of public recognition; however, they were well represented by nearly every state in the union. On September 9, 1861, Company E was mustered into service, followed by Companies F and G, which were mustered in on November 28 and December 10, 1861. Companies F and G were assigned to the 2nd Regiment. Gen. Hiram Berdan's U.S. Volunteer Sharpshooters were involved in 36 engagements, including Gettysburg, Cold Harbor, and the Wilderness.

Illustrated is a sharpshooter on picket duty, by artist Winslow Homer. Sharpshooters played an important part in the operations of the army. Hiding themselves in a good position, they soon built a little pit, digging with a bayonet and tin cup.

SHARPSHOOTING, TRIAL OF SKILL, BERDAN'S RIFLEMEN. Gen. Hiram Berdan organized the famous corps of crack riflemen known as the 1st and 2nd Regiments of the U.S. Sharpshooters, of which New Hampshire men were members during the Peninsular Campaign of 1862. Here, the sharpshooters are being trained and tested; most of them in the rank could score a bull's eye every time. Of the 2,570 sharpshooters, 1008, or 40 percent, were killed or wounded during the war.

PVT. NATHAN MORSE. Morse served in Company F, 2nd Regiment, Berdan's New Hampshire Volunteers, and in Berdan's U.S. Sharpshooters. None of the sharpshooters received extra, none were reimbursed for using their own weapons, and none were exempt from battle duty.

PVT. HENRY A. BEDFIELD. Bedfield served in Company G, 2nd Regiment, Berdan's New Hampshire Volunteers, and in Berdan's U.S. Sharpshooters. The only promise that Berdan gave his recruits was that each would receive Sharps rifles.

NEW HAMPSHIRE AND THE U.S. NAVY: "THE WORLD'S MOST POWERFUL." The U.S. Navy was little prepared for the advent of the Civil War. Many of its commissioned vessels were obsolete, and most were stationed in foreign ports. In home ports, only four warships were available for duty, and most of the trained seamen came from the coast of New England. According to naval records, the United States owned 90 ships that carried 2,415 guns at the beginning of the war; the 42 commissioned vessels in the fleet carried only 555 guns. The need for ships to enforce the blockade of the 3,000-mile-long Confederate coast required the Union to secure hundreds of new ships.

Gradually, the navy tightened its blockade of Confederate ports and, one by one, severed the South's commercial connection with foreign countries. By the end of the rebellion, the U.S. Navy was considered the foremost naval power in the world. The Civil War had revolutionized the science of naval warfare through its new technology, thus making other navies throughout the world obsolete.

REAR ADM. JOHN A. WINSLOW, CAPTAIN OF THE *KEARSARGE*. Captain Winslow and his crew of mainly New Hampshire seamen found the Confederate ship *Alabama* in the harbor of Cherbourg, France. On Sunday morning, June 19, 1864, the *Alabama* steamed out of the harbor amid the plaudits of thousands of Englishmen and Frenchmen, who had no doubt that she was going to certain victory. Winslow directed the *Kearsarge* away as the *Alabama* approached and drew it off to a distance of seven or eight miles from the coast. He then turned and closed in on the enemy.

CAPT. JOHN A. WINSLOW AND THE OFFICERS ON THE DECK OF THE MAN OF WAR USS KEARSARGE. In 1861, a declaration of war was issued and the Union navy made ready to authorize the construction of 16 large sloops of war, including the USS *Kearsarge*, which was named for one of New Hampshire's mountains, Mount Kearsarge. In January 1863, the 1,031-ton *Kearsarge* was commissioned. The vessel carried sails on three masts to supplement the steam-powered screw propeller. With a length of 200 feet, it was designed to be narrow and shallow so as to achieve maximum speed against the enemy. The vessel was supplied with 8 guns, including two 11-inch Dahlgren pivot guns mounted amidship, which would allow it to rake large areas with 135-pound shots. The flank of the *Kearsarge* was protected by a set of 32 pounders, and its gunners were famous for their superior skill.

For one year, Captain Winslow chased after the Confederate ship CSS *Alabama*, and when he learned that the Rebel ship was lying at the harbor in Cherborurg, France, seeking repairs, he headed off in pursuit. "The contest will no doubt be contested and obstinate, but the two war ships are so equally matched that I do not feel at liberty to decline it," remarked Captain Semmes of the *Alabama*, when the *Kearsarge* came within sight.

THE 11-INCH FORWARD PIVOT GUN ON THE USS KEARSARGE IN ACTION. The two vessels steamed around on opposite sides of a circle half a mile in diameter, firing their starboard guns. The practice on the *Alabama* was very bad; it began firing first, discharging its guns rapidly, and producing little or no effect, although a dozen of its shots struck the *Kearsarge*. But when the *Kearsarge* began firing, as seen here, this was war in earnest. Its guns were handled with great skill, and every shot hit its mark. One of them cut the mizzenmast so that it fell. Another exploded a shell among the crew of the *Alabama*'s pivot gun, killing half of the men and dismounting the piece.

THE OPENING OF THE BATTLE BETWEEN THE *KEARSARGE* AND THE *ALABAMA,* JUNE 19, 1864. Balls rolled in at the portholes and swept away the gunners of the CSS *Alabama,* and several pierced the hull below the waterline, making the ship tremble from stem to stern, thus letting in the flood of water. The vessel had described seven circles, and the *Alabama's* deck was strewn with the dead when, at the end of the hour, the boat was found to be sinking, and the officers, with a keen sense of chivalry, threw into the sea the swords that were no longer their own.

THE SINKING OF THE CSS *ALABAMA,* JUNE 19, 1864. The USS *Kearsarge* lowered boats to take off the crew, but suddenly the stern settled, the bow was thrown into the air, and down went CSS *Alabama* to the bottom of the British Channel, carrying an unknown number of her men. An English yacht picked up Captain Semmes and some 40 sailors and steamed away to Southampton; others were rescued by the boats of the *Kearsarge;* some drowned.

THE BOAT OF THE *DEERHOUND* RESCUES CAPTAIN SEMMES. Captain Semmes struck his colors, and at 12:24 p.m., after 90 minutes of battle, the CSS *Alabama* disappeared beneath the waves.

Semmes in his official notes indicated the following: "At the end of the engagement it was discovered, by those of our officers who went alongside the enemy's ship with the wounded, that her midship section on both sides was thoroughly iron-coated. The planking had been ripped off in every direction by our shot and shell and the chain broken and indented in many places, and forced partly into the ship's side. The enemy was heavier than myself, both in ship, battery, and crew; but I did not know until the action was over that she was also iron-clad."

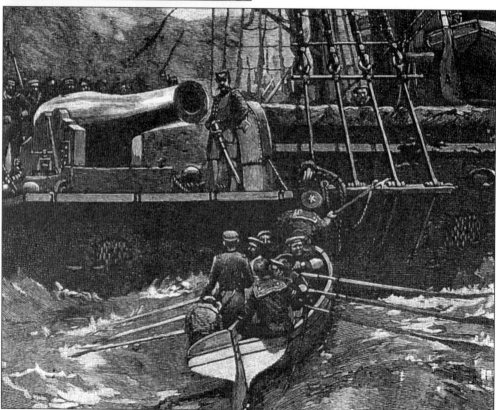

THE BOAT FROM THE *ALABAMA* ANNOUNCING THE SURRENDER AND ASKING FOR ASSISTANCE. This picture shows shot marks in the covering of the chain armor amidship.

Two

CAMP LIFE

THE 1ST NEW HAMPSHIRE REGIMENT CROSSING PLEASANT ON MAIN STREET, CONCORD.
When the Civil War began, there was throughout the state a great uprising. Men volunteered
by the fifties, hundreds, and by the thousands. They were sent to camps, where they were
organized into regiments and prepared for training.

THE ARRIVAL AND DEPARTURE OF THE UNION TROOPS EN ROUTE TO THE FRONT LINES (1861–1862), THE UNION VOLUNTEER REFRESHMENT SALOON, PHILADELPHIA. This metropolis was not infected with the sentiment of secession. Union soldiers were greeted and prepared for battle at this stop. They had a gala day. They were met and welcomed by crowds in the thousands. Bands played and supplies were handed out. Then the soldiers were sent on their way.

THE UNION VOLUNTEER RESTAURANT, PHILADELPHIA, WHERE SOME 900,000 UNION SOLDIERS WERE FED. This is the great Union barracks refreshment saloon, with a train of the Philadelphia, Wilmington & Baltimore Railroad, from which the incoming volunteers had dismounted. The Stars and Stripes flew proudly above the barracks.

72

THE QUARTERS OF CAPTAIN WIGGINS, HILTON HEAD, SOUTH CAROLINA, MARCH TO APRIL 1862. The officers in this picture are playing a game of dominoes in front of the captain's tent. The officers are Pierce Wiggins, George Emmons, Michael Donohue, and Henry Handerson.

A GROUP OF COMPANY H, 3RD NEW HAMPSHIRE VOLUNTEER REGIMENT, HILTON HEAD, SOUTH CAROLINA, MARCH TO APRIL, 1862. These enlisted men are enjoying a light moment of conversation and refreshment.

THE 3RD NEW HAMPSHIRE BAND, HILTON HEAD, SOUTH CAROLINA. This band was organized at Concord and was mustered into service on February 10, 1863, under the direction of Gustavua W. Ingells of Concord. The band was stationed at Hilton Head, South Carolina, and was held in high esteem by the commanding officers.

THE REGIMENTAL BAND IN FORMATION, HILTON HEAD, SOUTH CAROLINA. "I can assure you, that you and every member of your Band, stands in the highest estimation of every one in this department from Major General Gilmore down. We never expect to see such another as Ingell's Post Band here again." Signed: W.T.M. Burger, Assistant Adjutant General, Hilton Head, South Carolina. The band was mustered out on July 4, 1865.

THE HEADQUARTERS, COMPANY E, 18TH NEW HAMPSHIRE VOLUNTEERS, CITY POINT, VIRGINIA, 1864–1865. Shown is W.A. Gile, captain, commanding Company E, 11th New Hampshire Volunteer Regiment.

DR. SAMUEL P. CARBEE. Samuel Carbee was the regimental surgeon for the 12th New Hampshire Volunteer Regiment. The majority of New Hampshire surgeons, such as Carbee, were compassionate men who conscientiously performed their duties under very difficult condition. The Union medical records of surgeon casualties indicate the extent of the doctors' dedication and the risks they took to help their men: surgeons killed in battle numbered 42, those wounded numbered 83, and those who died of disease or accident numbered 290.

PNEUMONIA AFFLICTED THE WEAK. With only tents to protect against the cold and snow, the men faced increased risk of pneumonia in this 1863 Virginia camp. Most soldiers had less to fear from bullets than from disease. During these war years, physicians did not know that pneumonia was often caused by viruses, fungi, and bacteria, or that even contaminated dust could be taken into the system and affect a very healthy soldier. One affected Yankee soldier wrote, "The Regtl. Surg., our Chaplain & my Son done all they could for me. They kept me hot bricks to my feet & hot cloths on my stomach but the Cold clamy Sweat ran out at every poar cold as death. Oh such hours of suffering, but the Lord was with me praise his holy name."

THE COOK'S GALLEY FOR COMPANY H, 3RD NEW HAMPSHIRE REGIMENT, HILTON HEAD, SOUTH CAROLINA, 1862. Meals for the soldiers were commonly prepared in company quarters and distributed to the men. This system prevailed where soldiers were permanently stationed in camps and lived in barracks, as seen here in Hilton Head, South Carolina.

THE SOLDIERS' DIET. Pictured is a typical campsite where New Hampshire soldiers would gather around the makeshift campfire and cook whatever was available from government issue, from peddlers, or from the land itself.

Needless to say New Hampshire soldiers suffered from poor diets and, consequently, from poor health. The lack of fresh fruits and vegetables led to rampant scurvy among the troops. Eating raw and rotten meat often produced digestive disorders. Most soldiers did their own cooking by frying everything. With little cooking experience and few ingredients, some unique dishes were created. Coosh, or slosh, was cornbread, cornmeal, or flour mixed with water until the mixture flowed like milk. It was fried in boiling grease until the water boiled off and then it resembled dirty brown hash. Ash cakes were made of cornmeal mixed with salt and water, and then wrapped in cabbage leaves and cooked in the ashes until firm. Sometimes dried vegetables were doled out to the soldiers in two-inch-thick cakes. Called "desecrated vegetables" or "baled hay" by the soldiers, the cakes looked like a "dirty brook with dead leaves floating around" when mixed with water.

THE LIBBY PRISON, RICHMOND, VIRGINIA, AUGUST 23, 1863. Probably no spot identified with war is more familiar by name than the celebrated Libby Prison in Richmond. Some of its importance in the annals of war is derived from the fact that only commissioned officers were imprisoned there. The privations to which these men were subjected during their incarceration in the middle of a thriving city have made the story of Libby Prison a tragedy.

THE LIBBY PRISON, RICHMOND, VIRGINIA. The prison stood on the Lynchburg Canal, near the James River, in the heart of Richmond. Formerly a ship chandler's warehouse, it was built of brick, was 105 feet by 140 feet on the ground floor, and was divided into nine rooms, each 45 feet by 105 feet. Here, the prisoners were packed in, far beyond the capacity of the quarters. Many thrilling escapes were effected by the prisoners, the most notable being that of Colonel Rose's tunnel, which was dug underground from the farther end of the building, as shown in the picture, by means of which about 100 officers got out of the building, half of whom reached the Union lines in safety.

Three
THE NEW HAMPSHIRE CIVIL WAR VETERANS' ASSOCIATION CAMPGROUND

THE NEW HAMPSHIRE VETERANS' ASSOCIATION CAMPGROUND MAIN GATE, WITH THE OLD HOTEL WEIRS (BACKGROUND). The New Hampshire Veterans' Association is the natural outgrowth of the camaraderie that binds men and women together in time of war, and of the desire to perpetuate that friendship in days of peace. The idea of forming this unique body—the only one of its kind in the United States—grew out of regimental organizations formed after the Civil War. The association was formed in 1875, primarily of Civil War veterans. One of the main purposes was to hold annual reunions during the summer months to renew the ties of fraternity, friendship, and loyalty that had been forged in the camps, hospitals, prisons, and on the battlefields. Articles of incorporation were granted by an act of the General Court of New Hampshire on July 7, 1881. When originally organized, the membership of the association consisted of men who had served in the Union forces on land and sea during the Civil War. All veterans, residents in New Hampshire, who have served in the armed forces of the United States since then are eligible for membership.

THE VETERANS' BUILDINGS ON LAKESIDE AVENUE, WEIRS, 1930S. The site chosen as a home for the New Hampshire Veterans' Association would have been hard to duplicate in this or any other state. Soon after 1870, the Methodists commenced holding summer camp meetings at the Weirs and, in 1879, the New Hampshire Veterans' Association held its first annual reunion here. The 7.7 acres of land now occupied by the association at the Weirs and within the city limits of Laconia slope upward from Lake Winnipesaukee. The association was given this land by the Boston, Concord & Montreal Railroad; however, it was not deeded to the association until 1924. The property offers a beautiful view of both the lake and the White Mountains beyond.

THE NEW HAMPSHIRE VETERANS' ASSOCIATION HEADQUARTERS, WITH THE BAND, 1880S. The construction of permanent camps for the various Civil War regiments, as well as a headquarters building, began during the 1880s and 1890s. By the 1920s, many of the Civil War veterans were no longer living, but the New Hampshire Veterans' Association became revived by the infusion of World War I veterans and, eventually, veterans of all wars. The number of buildings in Veterans Grove has declined. During the 1920s, there were as many as 35 structures on the property, but today only 15, mostly late-19th-century architecture.

The first floor of this building consists of a large meeting room with offices to the side and rear. On the second floor is a large meting room with smaller rooms to the rear. The third floor houses a dormitory and storage area.

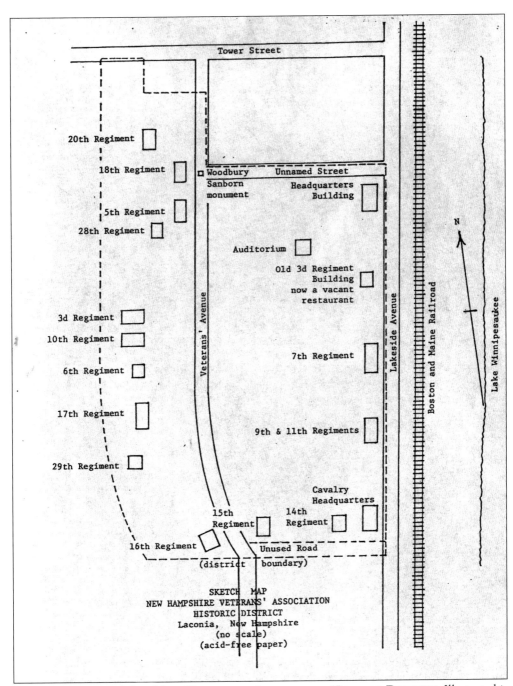

THE CAMPGROUND MAP, NEW HAMPSHIRE ASSOCIATION HISTORIC DISTRICT. Illustrated is a map of the New Hampshire Veterans' Association Campground, indicating the location of each regimental building on the hillside west of Lakeside Avenue at Weirs Beach.

THE HEADQUARTERS OF THE NEW HAMPSHIRE VETERANS' ASSOCIATION. This property belonged to the Boston & Maine Railroad when first occupied by the New Hampshire Veterans' Association and was leased to it for 43 years. Then the General Court, by making adequate appropriations for it, enabled the association to buy the entire tract of land from the railroad. This it did in 1924 for the sum of $4,000. It now belongs to the NHVA and has only one proviso attached, namely: "That whenever said corporation, from any cause, shall become extinct and cease to exist as a corporation, then all the property, real, personal, or mixed, shall be and become the property of the State of New Hampshire to be used and expended by said State for charitable purposes and none other."

THE HEADQUARTERS BUILDING AT THE CORNER OF VETERANS AVENUE, C. 1895. Pictured, from right to left, are the headquarters buildings of the 3rd, 7th, and 11th regiments and of the cavalry (at the corner of Cavalry Street to the extreme left). In 1885, nine building lots were allotted to the following: No. 1 building site was headquarters, and consecutive lots were for the 3rd and 7th Regiments, the Cavalry, the 11th, 6th, 8th, 15th, and 16th Regiments. It is said that these buildings had running water and sewerage long before other summer camps in the Weirs area.

THE MEMORIAL STONE AT THE VETERANS' GROVE, THE WEIRS. On the hill is the Woodbury Sanborn Memorial. This stone was inscribed in 1882 with the names of every New Hampshire organization that went into the Civil War. The stone was surrounded in 1883 by a cast-iron and wrought-iron fence featuring pickets of cast-iron muskets—complete even to lock, ramrod, and bayonet—with cornerposts of vertical iron cannons, topped by cannonballs. Below the hill is a similar stone bearing tablets commemorating achievements of the veterans of the Spanish-American War and the world wars. According to Ray Young, author of *The Phantom 17th*, "It is the state's only memorial to what one may call a phantom regiment that never really existed and to a man, Col. Henry O. Kent, Commander of the 17th NH Volunteer Infantry, whose wartime service would have earned him fame and a medal, if performed at a later time during another war."

THE NEW HAMPSHIRE 2ND VOLUNTEER REGIMENT BUILDING. This was probably the second veterans encampment, built in 1879. That was the year before the railroad company made available the land that comprises the New Hampshire Veterans' Association grounds. During the 1990s, the building was taken down for safety reasons.

THE NEW HAMPSHIRE 3RD VOLUNTEER REGIMENT BUILDING. This building was constructed for the 3rd Regiment and First Band in 1885. Both the first and second floors had open areas that could be divided into two rooms. A third of the building was used by the band. This structure burned in 1924.

THE NEW HAMPSHIRE 5TH VOLUNTEER REGIMENT BUILDING. The 5th Regiment building was constructed next to the Lowell building in 1883. Located on the first floor is a large reception room. On the second floor are partitioned sleeping quarters.

THE NEW HAMPSHIRE 7TH VOLUNTEER REGIMENT BUILDING. This structure was completed in 1885 on Lakeside Avenue. The first floor consists of a large reception room. The second floor consists several sleeping quarters and a women's reception room.

THE NEW HAMPSHIRE 9TH AND 11TH VOLUNTEER REGIMENT BUILDINGS. In 1888, the 9th and 11th Regiments worked together to construct their building on Lakeside Avenue between the Cavalry and 7th Regiment buildings. On the first floors, two large reception areas were separated by folding doors with a fireplace at the ends of the room. The second floor is divided into two sections, which are subdivided into three rooms. Located on the third floor is an area used as dormitory space.

THE NEW HAMPSHIRE 8TH AND 13TH VOLUNTEER REGIMENT BUILDINGS. In 1889, one of the temporary barracks next to the 5th Regiment was converted for used of the 8th and 13th Regiments. When the devastating Hurricane of 1938 roared through New Hampshire, more than 200 pines came down, destroying the 8th and 13 Regiment National Veterans' speakers stand, convention pavilion, and a few smaller structures in the campground. The 14th Regiment, Cavalry, dining pavilion, and other buildings suffered some damage from the storm.

THE DINING PAVILION, 1880s. This wooden structure served more than 1,500 diners per day during reunion week. A small sign reads, "Meals Served All Hours." Chowder was a favorite. In 1888, the caterer purchased 75 gallons of clams, 55 gallons of oysters, 300 pounds of fish, 957 gallons of milk, 16 barrels of potatoes, 2 1/2 barrels of pork, and 14 barrels of crackers.

THE NEW HAMPSHIRE 14TH VOLUNTEER REGIMENT BUILDING. Below the National Veterans' Association building and above the Cavalry Headquarters, the 14th regiment constructed its building in 1893. The road was named Cavalry Avenue. It marked the southern boundary of the property.

THE NEW HAMPSHIRE 15TH VOLUNTEER REGIMENT BUILDING. Opposite the 16th Regiment, on Veterans Avenue, the 15th Regiment finished their building in 1888.

THE NEW HAMPSHIRE 16TH VOLUNTEER REGIMENT BUILDING. In 1887, the 16th Regiment Headquarters was constructed on Veterans Avenue at the southern end of the property. The building consisted of a large reception room with smaller rooms on the first floor. The second floor consists of two large sleeping areas with two smaller rooms in the front towers. Next to the 16th was the pavilion and smaller storage buildings. This building burned in January 1995.

THE NEW HAMPSHIRE CAVALRY HEADQUARTERS BUILDING. On Lakeside Avenue, at the southern end on the Veterans' property, the 1st New Hampshire Cavalry built its headquarters in 1887.

BREDAN'S SHARPSHOOTERS AND THE HEAVY ARTILLERY COMPANIES, 1906. Both the Sharpshooter and the Heavy Artillery companies constructed the last of the large building on the campground. This building sat at the western boundary of the property in an area with the state barracks. In 1995, it was destroyed by fire.

THE NATIONAL VETERANS ASSOCIATION BUILDING. The building of the National Veterans Association of New Hampshire no longer exists. It was located down the hill and adjacent to the 15th Regiment Headquarters on Cavalry Street, the southern boundary of the campgrounds. In addition to losses from the fire of 1924 and the hurricane of 1938, several of the Veterans Association buildings have been lost to fire in recent decades.

THE NATIONAL VETERANS ASSOCIATION OF NEW HAMPSHIRE BUILDING. In 1944, an auxiliary was formed as the New Hampshire Veterans Association Auxiliary. A section of the NHVA bylaws read as follows: "There shall be an Auxiliary to the NHVA known as the NHVA Auxiliary, made up of wives, mothers, daughters, and sisters of veterans who have served faithfully in the aforementioned services of the United States, and who have received an honorable discharge therefrom, and of Sons of Veterans organizations in the NHVA, also members of Auxiliary bodies of organizations participating in the NHVA."

THE MANCHESTER VETERANS BUILDING. In 1886, the 2nd Regiment and Manchester House (Grand Army of the Republic) were built to the right and rear of the Lowell building. A huge dining pavilion occupied the area in front and to the right of these structures out to Tower Street. Most of the buildings were very colorful and ornate in depicting the Victorian and Queen Anne camp architecture—balloon construction style, with sweeping roof lines and wraparound porches, adding an elegance and refinement typical of the period.

THE NEW HAMPSHIRE STATE BUILDINGS, C. 1895. Hastily erected in the three weeks prior to the 1881 reunion, five new barracks provided shelter for 1,000 men. Financed by the state, these simple structures were arranged in a semicircle above the amphitheater in the Veteran's Grove. Many of the buildings boasted running water and sewer facilities long before other camps in the region. Most structures featured large open areas on the first floors with fireplaces and water closets. The second and third floors consisted of dormitory-style sleeping quarters which could, in some cases, be broken up into smaller more private areas with partitions.

THE LOWELL VETERANS ASSOCIATION OF THE NEW HAMPSHIRE VETERANS ASSOCIATION BUILDING. The buildings on the property include regimental and veterans association houses. When the land was first acquired, tents were used and the first permanent building was erected by the Lowell Association, which was made up of New Hampshire soldiers. After this, land was plotted out for the different regiments and the first headquarters building was erected on the hill where the Manchester building stood.

THE SPEAKERS STAND AND AUDITORIUM, VETERANS GROVE. This property once held a large open-air auditorium with a seating capacity of more than 2,000. The outdoor auditorium occupied the entire hillside, with the regimental buildings arranged around the outer rim. The speaker's platform has held many famous men and women. A glance at past programs reveals the names of Grant, Sherman, Sheridan, Roosevelt, and many others who made military and naval history.

PRES. THEODORE ROOSEVELT SPEAKING AT VETERANS GROVE. Crowds, variously estimated at between 20,000 and 40,000, thronged the Weirs for a two-hour visit by the president on August 28, 1902. As reported by the *New York Times*, "The President's speech at the park where the veterans were gathered, was most favorably received. He stood on a table at the extreme end of the platform, and his athletic figure made him strikingly conspicuous."

THE GRAND ARMY OF THE REPUBLIC BANDSTAND. The heightened activity of the Civil War Veterans in New Hampshire during the late 1800s paralleled a dramatic increase in veteran social and political activity elsewhere in the country. In particular, the Grand Army of the Republic (GAR), a national association for Union veterans, was then entering a period of phenomenal growth. In the late 1870s, Americans in general were swarming to join fraternal orders. GAR meetings, like those of other such organizations, incorporated ritual, in this case based on military life, and featured campfires and encampments. Through posts established at the local level, the GAR reached into even the smallest communities. By 1890, the organization served as the primary vehicle through which ex-soldiers spoke with a common voice. As the GAR's position strengthened, the statewide veteran's association simultaneously narrowed its focus, becoming almost exclusively preoccupied with its annual reunion and improvements to its encampment.

THE CEREMONIAL FIELD PIECE AND CREW ON LAKESIDE AVENUE, C. 1900. In the background is Castle Rest, on the hillside west of Lakeside Avenue in the campground. The development of reunion spirit gained momentum in the early 1870s. At this time, a number of regiments began to meet for formal banquets, sometimes at the expense of the hosting towns from which the soldiers had enlisted. As the decade progressed, veterans urged even wider fraternization, and in June 1875, the New Hampshire Veterans' Association was organized at Concord. Although membership was open to veterans of all wars, the organization's principal aim was "simply to cherish those fraternal feelings engendered among men who devoted four of the best years of their lives for the maintenance of the Union."

A SALUTE TO DISTINGUISHED VISITORS, 1880S. On more than one occasion, ceremonial salutes of firing cannons were provided and mock battles were conducted along Lakeside Avenue and in the Veterans grove.

Four
NEW HAMPSHIRE CIVIL WAR MONUMENTS

MANY MONUMENTS.
Shown are the Soldiers
Monuments in Alstead,
Antrim, Ashland, and
Derry; the Soldiers and
Sailors Monuments in
Lancaster; and the
Loammi Bean Fountain
in Weirs Beach.

*"Erected by the Town of Merrimack, May 1892, in memory of her soldiers —
sailors, 1861-1865." Inscribed on the die are the names of all soldiers and sailors
who served through World War I.*

SOLDIERS' MONUMENT
MERRIMACK BY THE RIVER

*On the grounds of the American
Legion building in Milton is this
statue which reads simply "Eli
Wentworth Post, No. 89, GAR.
1861-1865."*

TWO MONUMENTS. Here are the Soldiers and Sailors Monument in Merrimack, and the
Soldiers Monument in Milton.

Standing watch over the crossroads
at the center of Chester, is this
Civil War Soldier. The inscription reads
"In Honor of Our Country's Defenders,
1861-1865, The Men of Chester Who
Died in the War for the Union".

FARMINGTON.

In memory of the men of Goffstown,
who served as soldiers and sailors in
all American Wars. Erected in honor
of Captain Charles Stinson by his
grandson, Henry E. Parker, 1916.
Statue is located in the center of town.

Major Bedee's Civil War Statue
Meredith, New Hampshire

Soldiers' Monument, Putnam Park.
PETERBOROUGH.

SOLDIERS' MONUMENTS. Shown are the Soldiers Monument in Chester, the 12th Regiment of New Hampshire Volunteers Monument, with a statue of Major Bedee, and the monuments in Goffstown and Farmington. Depicted are an infantryman and reliefs of an artillery duel, a cavalry charge, and the sinking of *Alabama* by the *Kearsarge*. Also shown is the monument at Putnam Park in Peterborough.

THE LOAMMI BEAN FOUNTAIN. This Civil War Monument was erected at the New Hampshire Veterans Association Campground at the Weirs. The monument was dedicated to Loammi Bean, a 37-year-old volunteer who served with the 8th New Hampshire Volunteer Regiment for three months.

On October 27, 1862, after a brief tour of duty, Bean was killed in the Battle of George Landing, Louisiana. In his honor "and to the memory of thousands of other gallant soldiers who laid down their lives that the Union might be preserved," his daughter erected this monument, dedicated at exercises conducted by the 8th New Hampshire Volunteer Regiment Association on August 29, 1894. Unfortunately, this monument is no longer at the Weirs headquarters.

THE SOLDIERS MONUMENT IN MANCHESTER. This monument includes the statues of an infantryman, a sailor, a cavalryman, and an artilleryman, a relief of volunteers going off to war, and a trophy.

THE SOLDIERS MONUMENT IN CLAREMONT. This monument was erected in memory of those who served to preserve the union.

CIVIL WAR MONUMENTS IN NEW HAMPSHIRE

ALSTEAD - Soldiers Monument {Infantryman}
ALTON - Soldiers Monument {Infantryman}
AMHERST - Soldiers Monument {Infantryman}
ANTRIM - Soldiers Monument {Infantryman}
ASHLAND - Soldiers Monument {Infantryman}
BARNSTEAD - Soldiers Monument {Infantryman}
BENNINGTON - Soldiers Monument {Infantryman}
CANDIA - Soldiers Monument {Infantryman}
CHARLESTOWN - Soldiers Monument {Infantryman}
CHESTER - Soldiers Monument {Infantryman}
CLAREMONT - Soldiers Monument {Infantryman}
COLEBROOK - Soldiers Monument {Infantryman}
CONCORD - George H. Perkins {Statue of Commodore Perkins; reliefs of two Civil War naval battles}
CONCORD - Soldiers Monument - {Infantryman}
CORNISH - Soldiers Monument
CORNISH - Shaw Memorial {Relief}
CORNISH - Admiral David G. Farragut
DERRY - Soldiers and Sailors Monument {Infantryman and Trophy}
DOVER - Civil War Monument {Soldier. Flagbearer, Sailor and Infantryman}
FARMINGTON - Soldiers Monument {Infantryman and Relief of Artillery duel, Cavalry charge, Sinking of Alabama by the Kearsarge}
GOFFSTOWN - Soldiers Monument {Infantryman}
HAMPSTEAD - Soldiers Monument {Infantryman}
HAVERHILL - Soldiers Monument {Infantryman}
HENNIKER - Col. Leander W. Cogswell
HOPKINTON - Soldiers Monument {Infantryman}
JAFFREY - Soldiers Monument {Infantryman}
KEENE - Soldiers Monument {Infantryman}
LANCASTER - Soldiers and Sailors Monument {Infantryman}
LEBANON - Civil War Soldier {Infantryman}
LITTLETON - Soldiers and Sailors Monument {Infantryman}
LONDONDERRY - Soldiers Monument {Infantryman}
LYME - Soldiers Monument {Infantryman}
MANCHESTER - Soldiers Monument {Statue of Infantryman, Sailor, Cavalryman, Artilleryman, relief of Volunteers going off to war, and trophy}
MARLBOROUGH - Soldiers Monument {Statue of Soldier, Flag-bearer, and relief of battle scene}
MEREDITH - 12th Regiment New Hampshire Volunteers Monument with statue of Major Bedee {Infantryman}
MERRIMACK - Soldiers and sailors Monument {Infantryman}
MILTON - Soldiers Monument {Infantryman}
NASHUA - Soldiers and Sailors Monument {Statue of Sailor and Infantryman, Cavalry and Artillery trophies, relief of sinking of Alabama by the Kearsarge, allegorical relief of end of the war.}
NASHUA - Major General John Foster
NASHUA - USS MONITOR Plaque {Relief}
NEW LONDON - Soldiers Monument {Infantryman}
NEWPORT - Soldiers Monument {Soldier and Flagbearer}
PEMBROKE - Soldiers Monument {Infantryman}
PETERBOROUGH - Soldiers Monument {Infantryman}
PITTSFIELD - Soldiers Monument {Soldier and Flagbearer}
PLAISTOW - Soldiers Monument {Infantryman}
PORTSMOUTH - General Fitz John Porter {Equestrain statue relief of Battle of Malvern Hill and of General Porter in baloon}

A LIST OF CIVIL WAR MONUMENTS IN NEW HAMPSHIRE. "We fought in the War of 1861–1865 for the Preservation of the Union."

PORTSMOUTH - Soldiers and Sailors Monument {Statue of Infantryman and Sailor, relief of Parrot gun; sinking of Alabama by the Kearsarge, stack of muskets and a capstan.}
RAYMOND - Soldiers and Sailors Monument {Infantryman}
RINDGE - Memorial {Clara Barton relief, Memorial Bell Tower}
ROCHESTER - Soldiers Monument {INfantryman}
ROLLINGSFORD - Soldiers Monument {Infantryman}
SEABROOK - Soldiers Monument {Infantryman}
SPRINGFIELD - Soldiers Monument {Infantryman}
STODDARD - Soldiers Monument {Infantryman}
SUTTON - Soldiers and Sailors Monument {Infantryman}
TILTON - Soldiers Monument {Infantryman}
WARNER - General Walter Harriman
WARREN - Soldiers Monument {Infantryman}
WILMOT - Soldiers Monument {Infantryman}
WINCHESTER - Soldiers Monument {Soldier and Flagbearer}
WOLFEBORO - Soldiers Monument {Soldier and Flagbearer}
Ref: New Hampshire SOS files of War Monuments as provided by Mr. David Ruell, Ashland, NH.

"In Memory of the men of Stoddard who served as soldiers and sailors in all American Wars. Erected by James H. Hunt, Lieut. Co. G, 14th Regt. N.H. Vols. 1862-1865, 1917." The Stoddard Congregational Church in the background.

THE STODDARD MONUMENT. This view shows the Soldiers Monument in Stoddard.

THE CEMETERY STONES OF CIVIL WAR VETERANS. This view of the cemetery at Hilton Head, South Carolina, is a forcible reminder of an enemy more potent than bullet or shell: disease that thinned the ranks of the 3rd New Hampshire Volunteer Regiment before it faced the foe on the battlefield. Malaria was the known curse of the seacoast. The headboard in the foreground recalls a mournful episode of young soldier Amasee Niles, barely 17 years old, who died in a terrible storm while en route around Hatteras on the way to Port Royal.

THE GETTYSBURG MARKER, "NEW HAMPSHIRE / 49 BODIES." The army from New Hampshire, along with those from the other Northern states, fought for the possession of Gettysburg, and so there ensued a tempest of musket firing such as was not seen in any other engagement during the Civil War.

THE MEMORIAL OF THE 5TH NEW HAMPSHIRE REGIMENT. The inscription reads, "Grateful descendants of the heroes at Gettysburg erect beautiful and lasting memorials to the deeds of their soldier forebears at the scene of the greatest struggle of a now happily reunited nation."

DEVIL'S DEN AT THE GETTYSBURG NATIONAL BATTLEGROUNDS, GETTYSBURG, PENNSYLVANIA. One of the fascinating spots on the battlefield is today much as it was when terrible fighting took place in the crevices and sharpshooters and snipers fired from their vantage point behind the big rock. Today, Devil's Den is unchanged except for the bloom of a few trees in the springtime and the gathering of moss. Devil's Den was truly a Devil's Den during the three-day engagement at Gettysburg.

THE REUNION OF THE 12TH NEW HAMPSHIRE VOLUNTEER REGIMENT AT DEVIL'S DEN, GETTYSBURG, PENNSYLVANIA, 1890. Today, Devil's Den affords a bleak and weird picture. It

is located opposite Bloody Run from Little Round Top. Its huge boulders tower almost majestically, as though proclaiming immunity from the three-day battle.

THE SOLDIERS NATIONAL MONUMENT, GETTYSBURG, PENNSYLVANIA. This monument marks the spot in the Gettysburg National Cemetery, from which Pres. Abraham Lincoln delivered his immortal address at dedication ceremonies on November 19, 1863. Lincoln's dedicatory address consumed less than 10 minutes and, although deemed rather unimportant at the time, it echoed down through the years, a priceless reminder of America's heritage.

Five
IN MEMORY OF THOSE WHO SERVED

FRANKLIN PIERCE, 14TH PRESIDENT OF THE UNITED STATES, 1853–1857.
Franklin Pierce, an attorney and the son of a former governor of New Hampshire, entered Democratic politics at the age of 25. In 1853, when he became the 14th president, he was the youngest man to hold that office up to that time. Pierce strove to placate the South and promote harmony for the sake of economic prosperity. He opposed antislavery agitation. One of five living presidents at the start of the Civil War, Pierce was adamantly opposed to the prosecution of the war and the policies of the Republican administration of Pres. Abraham Lincoln. He died at his Concord home in 1809, four years after the end of the war.

WILLIAM PITT FESSENDEN, NEW HAMPSHIRE REPRESENTATIVE, SENATOR, ABOLITIONIST, AND ONE OF THE FOUNDERS OF THE REPUBLICAN PARTY. William P. Fessenden was born in Boscawan in 1806. He established himself as a man of great intellect, conviction, character, and ability. In 1840, he was elected to the U.S. House of Representatives and, in 1854, to the Senate. He never cared for life in Washington, and in the course of his career he became known for having a disagreeable personality and for being aggressively critical and insensitive. However, when the Civil War broke out, he was called upon to serve as a leader and cabinet member.

BENJAMIN FRANKLIN BUTLER. Born in New Hampshire and educated in Maine, Benjamin Butler became a successful criminal lawyer and a staunch Democrat and served in both houses of the Massachusetts state legislature. Butler's colorful military career began immediately after Fort Sumter.

When rioters in Baltimore prevented Union troops from being sent through that city to defend Washington, D.C., Butler's troops calmed the disturbance. For this Butler became Pres. Abraham Lincoln's first appointment to the rank of major general of the volunteers, one of the Union's "political generals," those men who owed their rank not to their political clout.

CHARLES ANDERSON DANA, SPECIAL AGENT FOR STANTON. Charles Dana was hired by War Secretary Edwin Stanton as an investigator and troubleshooter in 1862. As Stanton's agent, Dana spent much of the war at the front lines and sent frequent reports about the country's military leaders back to Washington. After his term of duty, Dana became an editor and part owner of the *New York Sun.*

| Gilman Marston, Colonel of the 10th Regiment. | Simon G. Griffin, Leader at the Crater Battle. | Joab N. Patterson, Colonel of the 2d Regiment. | Joseph H. Potter, Promoted for Gallantry. | John L. Thompson, Colonel of the 1st Cavalry. |

FEDERAL GENERALS—No. 13—NEW HAMPSHIRE

FEDERAL GENERALS OF NEW HAMPSHIRE. Pictured from left to right are the Union generals from New Hampshire: Gilman Marston, Simon G. Griffin, Joab N. Patterson, Joseph H. Potter, and John L. Thompson.

CAPT. WILLIAM W. MAYNE, COMPANY C, 1ST NEW HAMPSHIRE VOLUNTEER REGIMENT. William Mayne was a resident of Manchester who enlisted at the age of 21 on April 20, 1861. He was mustered in on May 2, 1861, as a corporal and was mustered out on August 9, 1861. He was transferred to the 4th New Hampshire Volunteer Regiment on August 19, 1861, as a private, was appointed second lieutenant, and was mustered in on September 18, 1861. On October 3, 1862, he was appointed captain. Wounded on June 29, 1864, near Petersburg, Virginia, he was discharged on September 14, 1864.

CAPT. MATTHEW ADAMS, COMPANY H, 4TH NEW HAMPSHIRE VOLUNTEER REGIMENT. Matthew Adams was born in Newbury and was a resident of New London. He enlisted on August 20, 1861, at the age of 19. He was mustered in on September 18, 1861, as a sergeant and was appointed second lieutenant on September 24, 1863. Wounded on July 30, 1864, at the mine explosion in Petersburg, Virginia, he was appointed captain of Company A on November 21, 1864. He was mustered out on August 23, 1865.

2ND LT. JOHN W. BREWSTER, COMPANY B, 4TH NEW HAMPSHIRE VOLUNTEER REGIMENT. John Brewster was a native of Portsmouth. He enlisted on September 13, 1861, at the age of 39. He was mustered in on September 18, 1861, as a corporal and was appointed sergeant. After being wounded on October 22, 1862, at Pocotaligo, South Carolina, he was appointed second lieutenant on December 1, 1862. He was wounded on May 20, 1864, at Drewry's Bluff, Virginia, and was discharged due to a disability on September 14, 1864.

DR. JAMES P. WALKER, ASSISTANT SURGEON, COMPANIES F AND S, 4TH NEW HAMPSHIRE VOLUNTEER REGIMENT. Dr. James Walker was a native of Manchester. Appointed second surgeon on May 2, 1864, at the age of 36, he was mustered in on May 15, 1864. He was discharged due to a disability on November 2, 1864, and was transferred to the 6th New Hampshire Volunteer Regiment as assistant surgeon on December 16, 1863. He resigned his commission on February 8, 1864.

WILLIAM H. THOMAS, CHAPLAIN, COMPANIES F AND S, 4TH NEW HAMPSHIRE VOLUNTEER REGIMENT. Rev. William Thomas was a resident of Laconia. He was appointed chaplain on October 23, 1863, at the age of 23. He was mustered in on November 16, 1863. He resigned on June 28, 1864.

CAPT. WILLIAM BADGER, COMPANY D, 4TH NEW HAMPSHIRE VOLUNTEER REGIMENT. William Badger, born in Gilmanton, was a resident of Sanbornton. He enlisted on July 25, 1861, at the age of 35 as a private. He was appointed captain on September 20, 1861, and was mustered in on September 18, 1861. On February 21, 1865, he was appointed colonel. Badger was a member of the 9th U.S. Veterans Volunteers and the 6th U.S. Infantry.

CAPT. DAVID O. BURLEIGH, COMPANY D, 4TH NEW HAMPSHIRE VOLUNTEER REGIMENT. David Burleigh was born in Sandwich and was a resident of Laconia. He enlisted on July 25, 1861, at the age of 40 as private. On September 18, 1861, he was mustered in as a second lieutenant. He was appointed first lieutenant on May 1, 1862, and captain of Company I on October 7, 1862.

CAPT. EPHRAM C. CURRIER, COMPANY K, 4TH NEW HAMPSHIRE VOLUNTEER REGIMENT. Ephram Currier, a native of Danville, enlisted on September 18, 1861, at the age of 27 as a private. He was mustered in on September 20, 1861, as a first lieutenant and was appointed captain on January 17, 1862. On August 12, 1862, he died of a disease.

CAPT. ISSAC W. HOBBS, COMPANY F, 4TH NEW HAMPSHIRE VOLUNTEER REGIMENT. Isaac Hobbs was born in Effingham and was a resident of Somersworth. He enlisted as a private on August 2, 1861, at the age of 24. On September 20, 1861, he was appointed first lieutenant. On December 1, 1863, he was appointed captain of Company A. He was wounded on July 18, 1864, near Petersburg, Virginia, and was discharged on November 7, 1864.

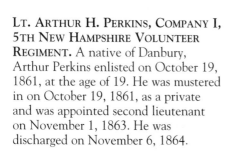

LT. ARTHUR H. PERKINS, COMPANY I, 5TH NEW HAMPSHIRE VOLUNTEER REGIMENT. A native of Danbury, Arthur Perkins enlisted on October 19, 1861, at the age of 19. He was mustered in on October 19, 1861, as a private and was appointed second lieutenant on November 1, 1863. He was discharged on November 6, 1864.

IRA STRAW JOHNSON, COMPANY K, 5TH NEW HAMPSHIRE VOLUNTEER REGIMENT. A native of Antrim, Ira Johnson enlisted on September 7, 1861, at the age of 18. He was mustered in on October 12, 1861, as a private. He was wounded on June 1, 1862, at Fair Oaks, Virginia, and was killed on December 13, 1862, at Fredericksburg, Virginia.

LT. COL. SAMUEL D. QUARLES, COMPANY D, 5TH NEW HAMPSHIRE VOLUNTEER REGIMENT. A resident of Ossipee, Samuel Quarles was appointed captain on November 30, 1861, at the age of 28. Wounded on May 18, 1864, at Spottsylvania, Virginia, he was appointed major on July 28, 1864, and lieutenant colonel on June 1, 1865. He was mustered out on July 17, 1865. He was appointed brevet lieutenant colonel, U.S. Volunteers, on April 2, 1865, for meritorious conduct before Petersburg, Virginia. He died on November 22, 1889.

1ST LT. GEORGE E. MUCHMORE, COMPANY E, 6TH NEW HAMPSHIRE VOLUNTEER REGIMENT. A resident of Keene, George Muchmore enlisted on October 17, 1861, at the age of 31 as a private. He was appointed second lieutenant on November 30, 1861. He was mustered in on November 28, 1861, was appointed first lieutenant on April 23, 1862, and was wounded on August 29, 1862, at Bull Run, Virginia. He died on September 11, 1862, in Washington, D.C.

2ND LT. ALVAH HEALD, COMPANIES A AND E, 6TH NEW HAMPSHIRE VOLUNTEER REGIMENT. A native of Temple, Alvah Heald enlisted on October 28, 1861, at the age of 19. He was mustered in on November 28, 1861, as a private. He was appointed corporal on January 1, 1864. He reenlisted and was mustered in on January 4, 1864. On June 1, 1865, he was appointed second lieutenant and was mustered out on July 17, 1865.

1ST LT. GEORGE F. ROBIE, COMPANIES D AND G, 7TH NEW HAMPSHIRE VOLUNTEER REGIMENT. George Robie was born in Candia and was a resident of Manchester. He enlisted as a sergeant on September 25, 1861, at the age of 18. He was appointed first sergeant on December 28, 1863. On February 28, 1864, he reenlisted, was mustered in, and was appointed lieutenant of Company G on October 28, 1864. He transferred to Company D and then to Company B on May 22, 1865. He was mustered out on July 20, 1865. Robie was awarded the Medal of Honor on June 8, 1883, under a resolution of Congress, No. 43, approved on July 12, 1862, and section 6 of an act of Congress, approved on March 3, 1863. The award was for bravery in 1864 at Richmond, Virginia.

PVT. JOHN R. SHERWIN, COMPANY B, 7TH NEW HAMPSHIRE VOLUNTEER REGIMENT. A native of Nashua, John Sherwin enlisted on September 24, 1861, at the age of 18. He was mustered in on November 1, 1861, as a private. Captured on February 20, 1864, at Olustee, Florida, he was released on December 30, 1864. He was discharged on April 17, 1865, in Concord.

PVT. FREDERICK W. SLEEPER, COMPANY C, 7TH NEW HAMPSHIRE VOLUNTEER REGIMENT. Frederick Sleeper was a resident of Plaistow. He enlisted on November 16, 1861, at the age of 19 and was mustered in on November 16, 1861, as a private.On July 18, 1863, he was wounded at Fort Wagner, South Carolina. He reenlisted, was mustered in on February 28, 1864, and was mustered out on July 20, 1865.

CPL. CHARLES M. NOYES, COMPANY F, 9TH NEW HAMPSHIRE VOLUNTEER REGIMENT. Charles Noyes, a native of Somersworth, enlisted on July 21, 1862, at the age of 21. He was mustered in on August 14, 1862, as a corporal. He was killed at Antietam, Maryland, on September 17, 1862.

CAPT. ORLANDO N. KEYES, COMPANY E, 12TH NEW HAMPSHIRE VOLUNTEER REGIMENT. Orlando Keyes was born in Hancock and was a resident of Holderness. He enlisted on August 19, 1862, at the age of 30 as a private. He was appointed first lieutenant on September 8, 1862, was mustered in on September 5, 1862, and was appointed captain of Company D on November 18, 1862. He was killed on May 3, 1863, at Chancellorsville, Virginia.

PVT. FREDOM SANBORN, COMPANY H, 12TH NEW HAMPSHIRE VOLUNTEER REGIMENT. Fredom Sanborn, a native of Sanbornton, enlisted on August 12, 1862, at the age of 20. He was mustered in on September 9, 1862, as a private. He was at Gettysburg, Pennsylvania, on July 2, 1863. He was discharged due to a disability on February 1, 1864. The following diary entry is taken from the archives of the Sanbornton historical records: "On August 12, 1862, enlisted in the 12 New Hampshire Regiment—was wounded at the Battle of Gettysburg on July 3, 1863, a ball passing through his throat and shattering his windpipe so as to prevent his speaking aloud for one year. As a farmer, he settled with his father at the bay. On October 1, 1873, at the age of 32, he died of a heart disease induced by his army experience."

CAPT. CHARLES O. BRADLEY, COMPANY C, 13TH NEW HAMPSHIRE VOLUNTEER REGIMENT. Charles O. Bradley was born in Hampstead and resided in Concord. On August 23, 1862, at the age of 26, he enlisted as a private. He was appointed captain on September 27, 1862. He resigned on June 10, 1864. Bradley also served in Company I, 1st New Hampshire Volunteer Regiment, as a first sergeant and captain.

2ND LT. S. MILLETT THOMPSON, COMPANY E, 13TH NEW HAMPSHIRE VOLUNTEER REGIMENT. S. Millett Thompson was born in Barnstead and was a resident of Durham. He enlisted on August 13, 1862, at the age of 24. Mustered in on September 19, 1862, as a first sergeant, he was appointed second lieutenant on June 10, 1863. After being wounded on June 15, 1864, at Battery Five, Petersburg, Virginia, he was discharged due to wounds on October 4, 1864.

REGIMENTAL SURGEONS SAMUEL A. RICHARDSON AND JONATHAN SULLIVAN, COMPANIES F AND S, 13TH NEW HAMPSHIRE VOLUNTEER REGIMENT. Samuel Richardson, born in Dublin, Ireland, was a resident of Marlborough. He was appointed assistant surgeon on September 16, 1862, at the age of 31 and was mustered in on October 4, 1862. Appointed surgeon on April 1, 1863, he was mustered out on June 21, 1865. Dr. Jonathan Sullivan Jr., a native of Exeter, was appointed assistant surgeon on September 16, 1862, at the age of 22, was mustered in on October 9, 1862, and was discharged due to a disability on August 16, 1864.

CHARLES A BROWN, COMPANY D, 15TH NEW HAMPSHIRE VOLUNTEER REGIMENT. Charles Brown, a native of Epsom, enlisted on September 17, 1862, at the age of 18. He was mustered in on October 8, 1862, as a private. He was wounded in service on May 27, 1863, at Port Hudson, Louisiana, and was mustered out on August 13, 1863.

CAPT. WILLIAM P. AUSTIN, COMPANY E, 1ST REGIMENT U.S. VOLUNTEER SHARPSHOOTERS. William P. Austin was born in Plainfield and was a resident of Claremont. He enlisted on August 9, 1861, at the age of 41. Appointed first lieutenant on August 17, 1861, he was mustered in on September 9, 1861, and was appointed captain on December 20, 1861. Austin was wounded on August 30, 1862, at Bull Run, Virginia, and was discharged on May 16, 1863.

PVT. CHARLES R. APPLIN, COMPANY F, 2ND REGIMENT U.S. VOLUNTEER SHARPSHOOTERS. Charles R. Applin was a native of Swanzey. He enlisted on October 2, 1861, at the age of 22. He was mustered in on November 26, 1861, as a private. He reenlisted on December 21, 1863, and transferred to the 5th New Hampshire Volunteer Regiment on January 30, 1865. Assigned to Company B on June 17, 1865, he was mustered out on June 28, 1865.

CAPT. ASEL B. GRIGGS, COMPANY F, 2ND REGIMENT U.S. VOLUNTEER SHARPSHOOTERS. Asel B. Griggs was a native of Orford. He enlisted on October 1, 1861, at the age of 24. He was mustered in on November 26, 1861, as a sergeant. He reenlisted on December 21, 1863, and was mustered in on December 25, 1863. He was appointed second lieutenant on May 11, 1864, and was wounded on June 22, 1864, at Weldon Railroad, Virginia. On November 22, 1864, he was appointed first lieutenant and on January 16, 1865, he was appointed captain. He transferred to the 5th New Hampshire Volunteer Regiment on January 30, 1865, and resigned on June 10, 1865.

State of New-Hampshire.

EXECUTIVE DEPARTMENT,

CONCORD, JULY 10, 1862.

To the People of New-Hampshire:

The alarming exigencies of the hour have induced the President of the United States to call upon the Executive of this State for three additional regiments, to be furnished at the earliest possible moment.

The President also desires that the regiments now in the service from this State, which have, by their noble conduct in every emergency, won imperishable laurels, and placed New-Hampshire high in rank among her sister States, be immediately recruited to the maximum standard.

The War Department has issued the following orders:

WAR DEPARTMENT, WASHINGTON, D. C.,
June 21, 1862.

Pursuant to a joint resolution of Congress to encourage enlistments in the regular army and volunteer forces, it is

Ordered, That a premium of two dollars shall be paid for each accepted recruit that volunteers for three years or during the war; and every soldier who hereafter enlists, either in the regular army or the volunteers for three years or during the war, may receive his first month's pay in advance, upon the mustering of his company into the service of the United States, or after he shall have been mustered into and joined a regiment already in the service. This order will be transmitted to Governors of States and recruiting officers.

(Signed,)   EDWIN M. STANTON, *Secretary of War.*

WAR DEPARTMENT, WASHINGTON, D. C.,
July 2, 1862.

Ordered, That out of the appropriation for collecting, organizing and drilling volunteers, there shall be paid in advance to each recruit, for three years or during the war, the sum of twenty-five dollars—being one fourth of the amount of bounty allowed by law; such payment to be made upon the mustering of the regiment to which such recruits belong into the service of the United States.

(Signed,)   EDWIN M. STANTON, *Secretary of War.*

In addition to the above inducements, the State of New-Hampshire will pay the further bounty of fifty dollars to each volunteer, upon his being mustered into the service. The above bounty of $50 will also be paid to recruits already enlisted into the 9th and 10th regiments.

Thus it will be seen that each volunteer will receive, cash in hand, upon being mustered into the service of the United States, the sum of ninety dollars ($90); also, at the expiration of his term of enlistment or honorable discharge from the service, he will receive the further bounty of seventy-five dollars ($75). In the event of his death the same will be paid to his family.

By the laws of this State, towns and cities will pay to families, and persons dependent on volunteers for their support, a sum not exceeding twelve dollars per month. (See act passed June session, 1862.)

All persons are further reminded that the sum of two dollars will be paid to any citizen or soldier for each accepted volunteer, and the Adjutant-General is hereby ordered to issue recruiting papers to such suitable persons as may offer their services as recruiting officers.

All men belonging to existing corps now in service, not under parole or disabled, are hereby notified that the orders of the War Department require their immediate return to their posts of duty. Colonel EASTMAN, of the U. S. Army—headquarters at Concord, N. H.,—upon application, will furnish all necessary facilities for transportation.

All good citizens are respectfully requested to report forthwith to the Adjutant-General of this State the name and residence of any volunteer or regular soldier of this State who may be evading his duty by not obeying the above order.

The Executive earnestly desires that the several towns and cities of the State forthwith adopt such measures as are recommended in the resolutions of the Legislature, passed at the recent session of the Legislature.

MEN OF THE OLD GRANITE STATE! Now TO THE RESCUE! Let not this call of your beloved Country ring through your hills and valleys in vain! Let there be a patriotic union of hearts and hands for the common weal, which shall not only preserve our ancient renown, and send a thrill of joy and exultation to our noble sons and brothers in the field, but shall also gladden the heart of the nation's Commander-in-Chief, and beckon our beloved loyal sister States to higher and still higher efforts for the salvation of our once happy, but now distracted country.

NATHANIEL S. BERRY, *Governor of New-Hampshire.*

TO THE PEOPLE OF NEW HAMPSHIRE. This comes from the state of New Hampshire to the people of New Hampshire and is dated June 21, 1862.

GENERAL ORDERS, } WAR DEPARTMENT,
ADJUTANT GENERAL'S OFFICE,
No. 232. } Washington, July 19, 1864.

FOR FIVE HUNDRED THOUSAND VOLUNTEERS.

By the President of the United States of America.

A PROCLAMATION.

WHEREAS, by the act approved July 4, 1864, entitled "An act further to regulate and provide for the enrolling and calling out the national forces, and for other purposes," it is provided that the President of the United States may, "at his discretion, at any time hereafter, call for any number of men, as volunteers, for the respective terms of one, two, and three years, for military service," and "that in case the quota of. [or] any part thereof, of any town, township, ward of a city, precinct, or election district, or of a county not so subdivided, shall not be filled within the space of fifty days after such call, then the President shall immediately order a draft for one year, to fill such quota, or any part thereof, which may be unfilled.;"

And whereas the new enrollment heretofore ordered is so far completed as that the aforementioned act of Congress may now be put in operation, for recruiting and keeping up the strength of the armies in the field, for garrisons, and such military operations as may be required for the purpose of suppressing the rebellion, and restoring the authority of the United States Government in the insurgent States:

Now, therefore, I ABRAHAM LINCOLN, President of the United States, do issue this my call for five hundred thousand volunteers for the military service; provided, nevertheless, that this call shall be reduced by all credits which may be established under section eight of the aforesaid act, on account of persons who have entered the naval service during the present rebellion, and by credits for men furnished to the military service in excess of calls heretofore made.

Volunteers will be accepted under this call for one, two, or three years, as they may elect, and will be entitled to the bounty provided by the law for the period of service for which they enlist.

And I hereby proclaim, order, and direct that, immediately after the

PROCLAMATION BY THE PRESIDENT. "General Orders No. 232, War Department: Adjutant General's Office, Washington, July 19, 1864." This is a request for 500,000 volunteers. Signed, A. Lincoln.

fifth day of September, 1864, being fifty days from the date of this call, a draft for troops to serve for one year shall be had in every town, township, ward of a city, precinct, or election district, or county not so subdivided, to fill the quota which shall be assigned to it under this call, or any part thereof which may be unfilled by volunteers on the said fifth day of September, 1864.

In testimony whereof, I have hereunto set my hand and caused the seal of the United States to be affixed.

Done at the city of Washington, this eighteenth day of July, in the year of our Lord one thousand eight hundred and sixty-four, and of the Independence of the United States the eighty-ninth.

[L. S.]

ABRAHAM LINCOLN.

By the President:

WILLIAM H. SEWARD,
Secretary of State.

BY ORDER OF THE SECRETARY OF WAR:

E. D. TOWNSEND,
Assistant Adjutant General.

OFFICIAL:

Assistant Adjutant General.

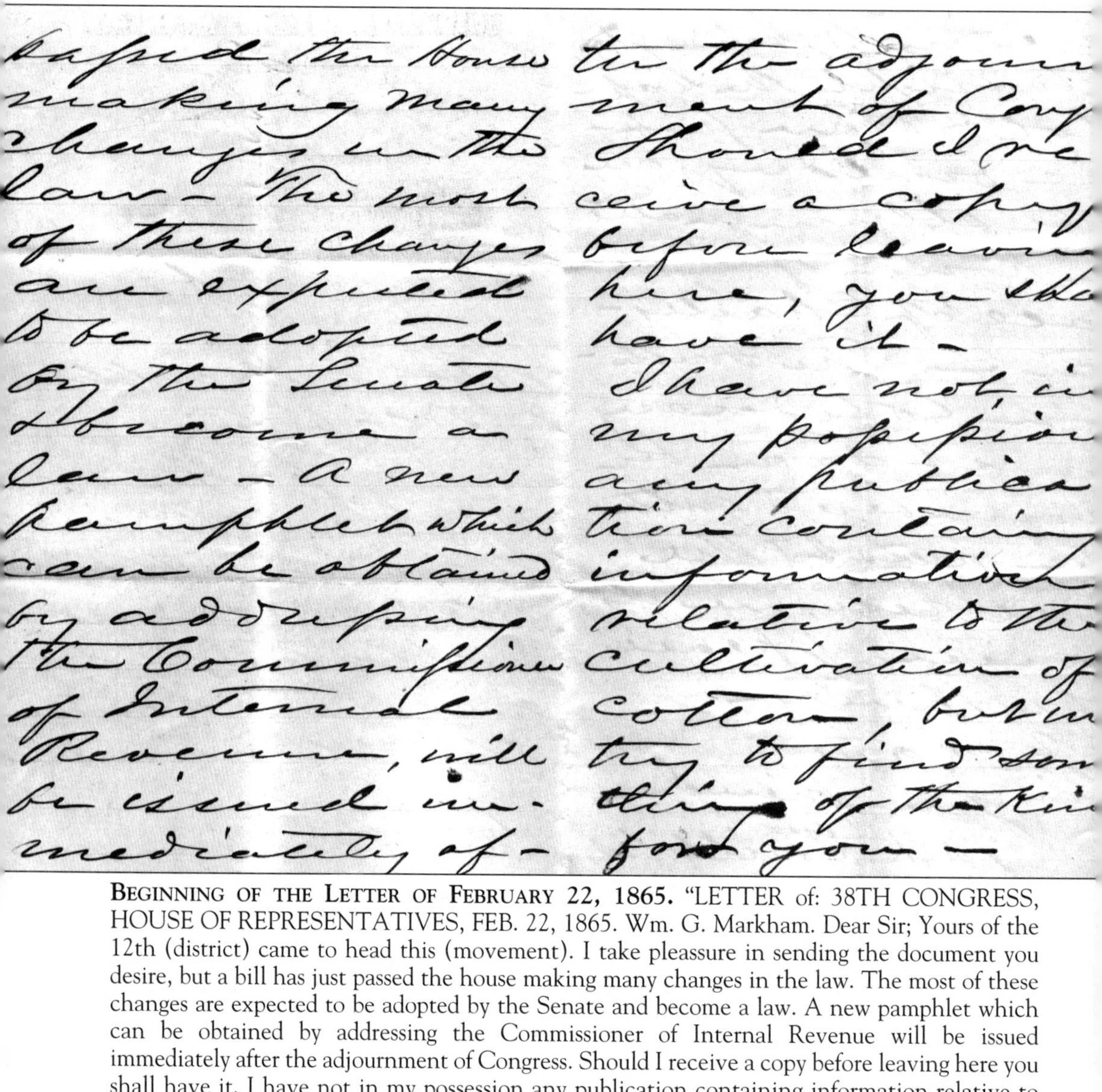
passed the House
making many
changes in the
law— The most
of these changes
are expected
to be adopted
by the Senate
& become a
law — A new
pamphlet which
can be obtained
by addressing
the Commissioner
of Internal
Revenue, will
be issued im-
mediately af-
ter the adjourn
ment of Cong
Should I re
ceive a copy
before leavin
here, you sha
have it —
I have not in
my possession
any publica
tion containing
information
relative to the
cultivation of
cotton, but wi
try to find som
thing of the kin
for you —

BEGINNING OF THE LETTER OF FEBRUARY 22, 1865. "LETTER of: 38TH CONGRESS, HOUSE OF REPRESENTATIVES, FEB. 22, 1865. Wm. G. Markham. Dear Sir; Yours of the 12th (district) came to head this (movement). I take pleassure in sending the document you desire, but a bill has just passed the house making many changes in the law. The most of these changes are expected to be adopted by the Senate and become a law. A new pamphlet which can be obtained by addressing the Commissioner of Internal Revenue will be issued immediately after the adjournment of Congress. Should I receive a copy before leaving here you shall have it. I have not in my possession any publication containing information relative to the cultivation of cotton but will try to find something of the kind for you."

[Handwritten letter, left column:]

Today is a joyful
one in Washington,
to night the Capi-
tol & other pub-
lic buildings are
to be illuminated
in honor of the
fall of Charles-
ton — The South-
ern Cofederacy
must soon be
numbered with
the past, the
Union will resume its
career of peace &
prosperity —
In haste,
your friend
M. D. Phillips.

[Handwritten letter, right column, on printed letterhead:]

UNITED STATES of AMERICA.

Thirty Eighth Congress

HOUSE OF REPRESENTATIVES,

Washington City Feb. 22 1865.—

Wm G. Markham
Dear Sir;
Yours
of the 12th inst
came to hand
this moment
I take plea-
sure in sending
the documents
you desire, but
a bill has just

ENDING OF THE LETTER OF FEBRUARY 22, 1865. "Today is a joyful one in Washington and tonight the capitol and other public buildings are to be illuminated in honor of the fall of Charleston. The Southern Confederacy must soon be (remembered) with the past, the Union will resume its careen of peace and prosperity. In (haste) your friend, M.D. Philips."

THE COST OF WAR, 1865. The total combined cost of the war for both the North and South has been estimated at more than $15 billion. In addition to the cost of lives, there was almost incalculable physical destruction of the South. Wrecked railroads and destroyed factories, towns, farms, and livestock added up an enormous loss best estimated by comparing property values. The 1860 census assessed the value of property in the South at $5.2 billion, but by 1870 its assessed value had decreased by 42 percent. Finding only ashes and devastation when they returned home, many Confederate veterans left the South in order to seek new opportunities for mere survival.